DISCOVERY!

LEARNING AND LIVING THE WILL OF GOD

a study in divine guidance by

KEN CHANT

with an interwoven story by Alison Chant

COPYRIGHT © 1991 BY KEN CHANT. ALL RIGHTS RESERVED WORLDWIDE P.O. BOX 79, WERRINGTON NSW 2747, AUSTRALIA

All rights in this book are reserved world-wide
No part of the book may be reproduced in any manner whatsoever without the written permission of the author except brief quotations embodied in critical articles or reviews

For information on reordering please contact:
Vision Publishing
1115 D Street
Ramona, CA 92065
www.visionpublishingservices.com
(760) 789-4700

ISBN # 1-931178-67-4

THIS BOOK IS BUILT UPON TWO PREMISES –

THE LORDSHIP OF CHRIST

and

THE AUTHORITY OF SCRIPTURE

CONTENTS

GETTING STARTED 7
CLEARING THE WAY 11

FIRST FALLACY 17
    GOD HAS A FIXED PLAN FOR MY LIFE!" 17
    Alison's Story 35
    WE LEARN OUR FIRST LESSONS! (1954-1955) 35

SECOND FALLACY 39
    I MUST GET GOD'S APROVAL BEFORE I DO
    ANYTHING" 39
    Alison's Story 57
    SAVED BY ANGELS! (1956) 57

THIRD FALLACY 63
    I CAN TEST THE WILL OF GOD WITH A 'FLEECE' 63
    Alison's Story 81
    SORROW TURNED TO JOY! (1955-1970) 81

FOURTH FALLACY 87
    OPEN DOORS REVEAL THE WILL OF GOD" 87
    Alison's Story 107
    THE HOLY SPIRIT TO THE RESCUE! (Adelaide 1957-
    1962) 107

FIFTH FALLACY 113
    GOD HAS A BLUEPRINT FOR MY MINISTRY!" 113
    Alison's Story 133
    WE MOVE TO TASMANIA (1963-1978) 133

SIXTH FALLACY 139
    I CAN MARRY ONLY THE SPOUSE GOD HAS

CHOSEN" 139
Alison's Story 157
GUIDANCE FROM ACROSS THE PACIFIC! (1974) 157

SEVENTH FALLACY **163**
"GUIDANCE COMES BY DIRECT REVELATION" . 163
Alison's Story 187
AN ADVENTURE FOR GOD! (Sydney & the USA,
1978-1982) 187

EIGHTH FALLACY **193**
"LOOK FOR THE APPROVAL OF TWO OR THREE
COUNSELLORS" 193
Alison's Story 209
MORE PRAYERS ANSWERED (1981-1986) 209

NINTH FALLACY **213**
"PROSPERITY SHOWS THAT I AM IN THE WILL OF
GOD" 213
Alison's Story 235
BACK TO AUSTRALIA! (1990-) 235

TENTH FALLACY **239**
"TRUE FAITH IS CONTENT TO STEP INTO THE
DARK!" 239

EPILOGUE **257**
A NEW BEGINNING 257
EXCEEDING ABUNDANTLY 260
ADDENDUM 273

Dr. Ken Chant

GETTING STARTED

George Gallup, of pollster fame, reckons that

> *"(the) strongest believers are those who believe because they feel God has intervened in their lives, that there are miracles, that there are meaningful coincidences, that there is a pattern to their lives, that God has a plan for their lives, that they've had miraculous prayers answered."*[1]

No evangelical Christian would dispute that description. God's guiding hand, answered prayer, supernatural intervention, a divinely ordained purpose for each believer - these are the very stuff of Christian life. If such things are not true, we may as well abandon our faith and become heathen again.

Yet that very confidence raises some difficult questions. We find ourselves trying to grasp two apparently opposing ideas. On one side, we assert our personal liberty, our God-given right of free choice. Yet on the other, we insist that God controls each Christian's destiny, which *"our times are in his hand"*[2]. So who *is* in charge? Does the outcome of your life depend more upon God's will or upon yours? Do *your* plans determine the shape of each new day, or do *his*?

Those questions inescapably lead to others:

---

[1] From an article, Tracking America's Soul, in "Christianity Today", November 17, 1989; pg. 23.
[2] Psalm 31:15. Robert Browning also used this phrase in the first stanza of his poem, "Rabbi Ben Ezra." You will find the full stanza quoted in chapter seven below.

- how willing is God to give you immediate and daily guidance?
- can you get instruction from the Father about the career you should follow, or the house you should buy?
- is it proper to ask God to prevent you from marrying anyone except the one spouse he has himself chosen for you?
- does the Lord really want to be involved in every decision you make, shaping and controlling your every choice?
- does he have a single plan for you to fulfill, only one path, and no other, that you can walk in obedience to his will?

Some Christians suppose there is a formula they can follow that will always bring a clear word from heaven. They hope to remove all doubt about what the Father wants them to do. Others reject the idea of supernatural guidance altogether, reckoning that God seldom, if ever, intervenes in human affairs.

Both of those positions seem too extreme. Does the Lord really invade our lives as often as some people claim? They talk as if they are in constant dialogue with God, receiving a flow of instructions from him on even the most trivial matters. Scant evidence exists, either in scripture or in life, to warrant such claims.

But the other error - denying altogether the possibility of guidance - is even more foolish. Who can doubt that divine shepherding is truly available to the Father's children? Scripture shows plainly enough that the Lord can and often does direct us - sometimes hidden, through circumstances; sometimes openly, through a miracle.

Yet the middle path between those extremes brings its own problems: when is it proper to expect heavenly regulation; when should we act upon our own initiative? If we are truly free, how can God be sovereign? If God is in control, how can we be free? If guidance *is* available from the Father, how can you discover it?

This book is an attempt to answer those questions. I have chosen to build it around ten popular ideas that become fallacies when they are pressed too far. Between each fallacy, my wife Alison has placed a story interlude, illustrating some of the ways the Father has guided us over the nearly 40 years of our marriage.

In a sense this book was anticipated long ago by that shrewd rabbi Sirach, who gave a fine summary of the matter in these words -

> *"Take advantage of every good opportunity that comes your way, while making sure to avoid any wrongdoing; and never be ashamed of the way God has made you."*[3]

One thing more. Across the years, while preparing myself to write other books, I have not hesitated to study deeply the Christian classics, and to utilize fully the wisdom and insight of other teachers. But about this book I could say with Sir Thomas Browne that it is

> *"not wrung from speculations and subtleties, but from common sense and observation -not pickt from the leaves of any author, but bred amongst*

---

[3] Sirach 4:20. Sirach was a Jewish rabbi, who flourished around 180 B.C. He wrote the book Continued from page 6...known as Ecclesiasticus, or The Wisdom of Sirach, one of the books of the Old Testament Apocrypha. It is a treasure of insight into the human condition.

the weeds and tares of mine own brain."⁴

Which means that, for better or worse, I have read hardly any book on the actual subject on divine guidance except the Bible and the pages of life. Whether that enhances or diminishes this volume you will have to determine for yourself.⁵

---

[4] Religio Medici I.36; written in 1643. Sir Thomas was a physician and astute observer of life.
[5] The scripture translations herein, unless another version is cited by name, are my own. The same is true of quotations from the Old Testament Apocrypha. To distinguish them from other sources, quotations from the Bible and from the Apocrypha are in italics. I do not, however, consider the books of the Apocrypha to be part of the inspired scriptures; although they are certainly useful for study and comparison.

Discovery

CLEARING THE WAY

Let's begin by ridding ourselves of a common fault: craving simple answers. Our generation is plagued by a loathing of the complex. Everywhere people are looking for an absolute formula, a clear rule, a plain solution of life's enigmas. Politicians campaign by promising absurdly facile remedies for enormously difficult problems. They offer slogans for substance. Electoral oblivion is sure to swallow any man or woman who in good conscience tries to be honest with the public. People prefer a spinner of fairy tales. No one wants to hear about the hard and hurtful surgery our ailing society really needs.

The church, too, is full of timorous simplifiers; lovers of microwave Christianity[6] who want every answer to be quick and easy. How thirsty these recipe-lovers are for delusion! How readily they reduce God to a platitude, insisting that all darkness become light, and all mysteries plain! Bewildered by complexity, distrusting ambiguity, afraid of awkwardness, terrified by uncertainty-these undaring saints, yearning to banish every shadow from life, eagerly snatch at any glib palliative.

Yet how can I criticize them? Am I not pushed by the same urge? Indeed, we all possess something of this ingrained reluctance to confront the harshness, the unfairness, that insistently clamors for our attention. As T. S. Eliot said: *"Human kind cannot bear very much reality."*[7] Were we to keep our eyes fully open, laughter

---

[6] A friend of mine in San Diego, Dr. Stan DeKoven inserted this phrase here ("microwave Christianity") when he read a rough draft of the above paragraphs.
[7] From his 1935 play Murder In The Cathedral, Pt. II.

would vanish from our days? If we did not block our ears, weeping would embitter every hour. Who could endure an unbroken contact with ugly injustice? Who could suffer without lull the cries of the hungry, the homeless, the tortured, the damned? So we allow ourselves to see and hear only a little, otherwise every hour would be a haunted nightmare, an intolerable burden of misery.[8]

Yet in these days of mass communication, reality is much harder to escape. Our forefathers rarely had to cope with tragedies any larger than those found in a single village or a small farming community. But we are confronted every day with images of mass terror, of multitudes of people devastated by all the ills that plague mankind. We were not built to withstand sorrow on such a monstrous scale -

> *"Open any volume of modern history, and the blood of innocents pours onto your hands. From government policies of starvation to countless varieties of religious wars, the 20th century is one huge Doomsday Book, a catalogue of horrors so vast that numbers lose human meaning. One death is a tragedy; millions of deaths are a statistic, to be deplored, then filed away as nightmares beyond comprehension. The atrocities nag at our conscience, finally numbing it. Amnesia seems the only solace."[9]*

So we blind our eyes; we dull our hearing; we learn to forget quickly; we stifle our compassion; and we go

---

[8] There is no fault in this self-protection, unless we carry it too far, refusing to see what we should see, or to hear what we should hear. Compare the parable of "Dives and Lazarus", Luke 16:19-31.
[9] Richard Corliss, in an article in "Time" magazine, January 8th, 1990.

searching for an easy answer. That is why, when Doug Marlette was asked, "Do people really want TV evangelists?" *he replied -*

> *"Yes. People want TV evangelists. They want gurus and answer people. They want simple solutions. They do not want ambiguity, and they do not want freedom, and they don't want a cross. They want someone else doing things for them."*[10]

THE GOD OF THE "BREAK-THROUGH"

But those "simple solutions" continue to elude us. The world refuses to respect our prejudice; it daily assaults us with its ugly reality. So we find that we must see and hear, we cannot turn away, there is no place to hide. This drives us to develop other evasive tactics, among which the most common is an attempt to rationalize the providence of God, to link every happening to some axiom of divine government, to restrict God to a set of human rules. So we decide for ourselves what the Lord will allow, and what he will prevent; we imagine that we know just what God will do and what he will not do. We demand a tidy God who does predictable things in a well-ordered world. "Perhaps this thing may happen to me," we say to ourselves, "but that one never will!"

But the Lord God laughs at our folly. He refuses to be enslaved by our pretensions. How silly to suppose that any earthly framework could ever limit the Glorious

---

[10] Doug Marlette is an editorial cartoonist and creator of the "Kudzu" comic strip. The above comment is taken from the Wittenburg Door, June/July 1987, pg 12. The context of the question was a discussion on the scandals that beset American TV evangelists in 1988/89, and on the inadequacies of television as a medium for presenting the gospel.

Creator, or that his ways and wisdom could be any more than dimly perceived by a human mind!

Instead, God compels us to share David's long-ago discovery that the King of Israel is "*Baal-Perrizim*", the Lord-Who-Breaks-Out-Upon his people.[11] He breeches the wall! No one can lock him into a neat little scheme. He casts off the flimsy shackles wrought by our dogmas! He does whatever he pleases in heaven and on earth![12] Astonishing us with innovation, confounding us with change, the Lord sternly trashes our logical theories and our comfortable programs.

Why do we even try to handcuff the God of infinite variety to a single pattern? Can the Source of all Wisdom be obliged to seek the approval of acolytes? Can the Father of a thousand cultures be compelled to applaud only the mores of one people? How fatuous to imagine that the way of one nation or of one church, of one family or of one person, of one civilization or of one society, is alone correct! How myopic to suppose that our view of the world is the only one approved by the Lord God!

Since we cannot padlock the Father behind the iron bars of human dogman, why not surrender now to the we see inevitability both of perplexity and surprise? Some things clearly, some darkly, and through it all, our God weaves a golden thread of delightful serendipity![13]

---

[11] 2 Samuel 5:20; 6:8; etc.
[12] Psalm 115:3; 135:6.
[13] "Serendipity" is a word coined by Horace Walpole in 1754, to describe the delightful things that kept on happening to the young heroes of his story, The Three Princes Of Serendip (Ceylon). It now has the idea of any unexpected good fortune, especially if the happy event occurs either when it is least expected, or when its timing is finely appropriate.

TRUTH HAS TWO SIDES

A final comment, before you turn to the First Fallacy. Both in scripture and in life there is an inescapable tension between the two sides of every truth. Thus the Bible contains a message of prosperity, but also one of poverty; of happiness, but also of tears; of triumph, but also of defeat. The art of Christian living is knowing each day on which side of the truth to stand; or, more bluntly, knowing when to change your mind! Indeed, every sensible person knows that it is quite possible to keep together several apparently contradictory opinions -

> *"The test of a first-class intelligence is the ability to hold two opposed ideas in the mind at the same time, and still retain the ability to function."* [14]

This paradox is merely a reflection of the general untidiness and ambiguity of all human experience. That is why the most dangerous people in the world are those with a single-minded obsession that blinds them to all other possibilities. But most ordinary people find themselves well able to look at things from several different viewpoints. Hence they are prone to shift from one opinion on a matter to another, depending upon what is presently influencing them.

Therefore I follow Paul's example. Today you might find me enjoying the abundance of the Lord, while tomorrow you would hear me welcome abasement in Christ. Today, by a miracle of answered prayer, I grasp everything; tomorrow I stand helpless while it is all stolen from me;

---

[14] F. Scott Fitzgerald; source unknown to me.

but on the day after, you might see me pray it all back again![15]

We all find ourselves facing multiple realities mixed in with a single event. Thus we look at a happening and at once find in it some things that make us happy, and some that make us sad. Which should we choose? Whichever is most appropriate for the moment! Or again, every day we are confronted by competing inadequacies, which clamor for preference. When every decision is a bad one, how can you make one that is right? But that is life.

So then does the Bible teach prosperity or poverty? It teaches both! The trick lies in knowing which one is right for you at the present time, and then being able to embrace that state by faith.

READ THE LAST CHAPTER FIRST

In harmony with these principles, although I have tried to maintain a balance of doctrine throughout the book, the following chapters (except for the last two) inevitably represent one side of Christian more than another. You might therefore find that you can keep the whole message of scripture in better focus if you read the last two chapters first, then read the ten Fallacies, *then read the last two chapters again.*

In any case, Alison and I pray with all our heart that through these pages you will truly learn how to live in a way that will always please the Father.

---

[15] See Philippians 4:12; also 1 Corinthians 4:11; 2 Corinthians 6:4-5; 11:23-28.

First Fallacy

GOD HAS A FIXED PLAN FOR MY LIFE!

A nun is praying in her room alone, happy in the love of God, confident of his help. A group of Guatemalan children will later be arriving at her school, and she is preparing to teach them. Suddenly her intercessions are shattered by a savage band of rebel soldiers. They burst into the room, beat her, strip her naked, mercilessly torture her, rape her many times, and leave her moaning and bloody on the floor. The children find her there. The terrible scene carves itself into their young minds, scarring with horror their nights and days.

With measureless joy a young father tells his friends at church that God has rescued his son from certain drowning on a South Australian beach. A strong current had carried the boy out to sea, and no one heard his cries for help. By mere chance - or so it seemed -a man walking along the beach glimpsed the small head dipping beneath the waves. He dived into the water, swam out, and brought the boy safely to shore. The lad's father says the hand of God was at work, protecting the family from heart-rending tragedy. He urges the church to give thanks with him for a miracle of divine protection.

A distraught husband rushes into a California schoolroom, puts two bullets into his estranged wife, then sexually assaults two other lady teachers who come to her rescue. The young women beg the sobbing children to turn their heads away from the shameful sight. People ask angry questions about divine justice. How can anyone say that *"God is love"* when he allows such vile things to happen?

Facing certain bankruptcy, an industrialist calls upon the Lord for help. Surely there is some way to save his business from ruin? At midnight he falls asleep, and in his dream sees detailed drawings of a clever way to improve one of his major machines. The invention is still clear in his mind when he awakes. It saves his company from ruin and turns him into a multi-millionaire. He shows his gratitude to God by giving munificently to charity and world missions, and everywhere he goes he tells people about the power of prayer and the goodness of God.

In the deep of night several bandits creep into an African mission compound. With axes they hack to death all the mission personnel, men, women, and children. The screams of the mutilated victims, and their frantic but futile cries for God's help, mingle with the callous and taunting laughter of their murderers. Other missionaries, terrified of suffering the same unspeakable death, abandon their stations and flee to safety.

> *"Doesn't God want the gospel proclaimed?"*, many ask. *"Why didn't he heed the cries of his servants? Perhaps he had a right to allow the adults to die as martyrs - but not those helpless children and babies! Why didn't he save them from being mangled?"*

Dying of cancer, a woman turns to her Bible and finds there a passage instructing her to call for the elders of the church. *"The prayer of faith,"* says James, *"will bring both salvation and healing to the sick person."* Hope leaps into her spirit. She has not been to church for a long time, but God might still show her mercy. She calls the elders, who come and anoint her with oil in the name of the Lord. She feels a great warmth sweep through her, and by morning the cancer is gone! God has given her a wonderful miracle![16]

Throughout the church and around the world the same scenes often occur. Everywhere, terrible acts of random violence are reported; yet alongside those stories come many others, telling about supernatural rescues and extraordinary divine protection. One person kneels trembling, appalled, asking with bitter sobs why God did not intervene. Another stands merrily, declaring how the Lord marvelously thwarted disaster and brought deliverance.

What are we to make of such things? Is there any pattern; are there any principles for us to learn?

EXCITING VARIETY

Seven times, scripture says, David *"enquired of God"* how to wage war against the Philistines.[17] Each time the Lord gave him a different strategy - now a handful of pebbles, then a sword; now the wind in the mulberry trees, then a frontal attack; now an ambush, then a siege. It was the *God – of – the - Breakthrough*:[18] unpredictable, exciting, majestic, awful, laughing at Israel's paltry plans, while exerting his own limitless wisdom and might.

---

[16] The above anecdotes are all based upon recent events.
[17] 1 Samuel 23:2,4; 30:8; 2 Samuel 2:1; 5:19,23; 21:1; plus parallels.
[18] 2 Samuel 5:20

Watch the Lord still earlier, when Israel invaded Canaan. Did he ever use the same tactic twice? No! Here trumpets bring down the city walls, there a mighty thunderstorm wins the battle; now terrible hailstones shatter the earth, but then stinging hornets rout the enemy! In one battle Israel triumphs by feat of arms; in another the voice of Yahweh roars from heaven and drives back the foe. No one can ever tell what God will do next!

We find this unsettling. We prefer constancy and conformity. We dislike an unpredictable Deity. Something in us abhors the grey and the shadowy. We crave a black and white scene, where all is clear, and nothing remains uncertain. How dismayed we are when some unexpected event shreds our neatly crafted structures! A freeway accident destroys one Christian family in the same week that a miracle saves another. We shake bewildered heads. We can't understand why things often don't work out the way we think they should. Surely something has gone terribly wrong? How can our system - those tidy rules we like to live by - prove so unreliable?

Yet here is the greater irony: we are far more often trapped by our own facile judgments than by any act of God. A large part of the mystery of life would disappear - or at least our questions would vanish - if we would only stop trying to force the Lord to live by our rules!

Instead, we are frequently like a pastor who came home from a vacation. After being met at the airport by a friend who was also a backslidden parishioner, the pastor asked if there were any news. His friend reported that a terrible fire had just swept through the neighborhood, and among the smoking ruins was his own house. He had lost everything he owned in the blaze.

"Aha!" cried the preacher. "I warned you that calamity would strike if you didn't repent!"

"Fair enough," the fallen saint admitted with rueful humility; "but here is some more bad news. The fire also reduced *your* house to a pile of ashes!"

The horrified minister hastily revised his opinion. "The ways of God," he lamented, "are indeed beyond understanding!"[19] He learned that divine providence seldom conforms to our prejudice! Which brings us back to our main question: is it possible to obtain a clear word from God about what you should do in every important issue of life? Given life's complexity, the plain answer is: no - although there are many exceptions.

Of course, I am not talking here about *moral* decisions. Scripture clearly tells how you and I should behave *ethically* and *morally*. No higher or better authority exists, and we are required to be immediately obedient to it. But what about those practical matters upon which the Bible is largely silent: your domicile, employment, spouse, church denomination, and the like?

ONLY A FEW CHOSEN

Perhaps you think there is only one pathway mapped out for you by God; only one person you can marry in the will of God; only one career you can righteously follow; only one town in which you are free to dwell; only one church you can obediently join?

---

[19] 1 Corinthians 13:9, 12. I think I first read this story in an old "Reader's Digest".

The Lord undoubtedly does have a fixed plan for some of his servants. What other choices, for example, were available to men like Abraham, Joseph, Moses, Jeremiah, Paul? They were all locked by the decree of God into a particular path. No doubt they each had much liberty within that path (thus Paul apparently felt free either to marry or not to marry, without offending the command of God)[20] - nonetheless, the fixed purpose of God for those men, and for many other people, both ancient and modern, is clear.

The same *may* be true for you; but it is unlikely. Think about the scriptures. Measure the long span of Israel's history and count the millions of its citizens. Across those centuries and out of that multitude, how many people did God mark for some unique purpose? Only a handful! Those few alone had a task so special they could not deviate from it without violating God's will. They were like Jeremiah: if they tried to cast off the divine yoke a fire burned in their very veins and drove them back to obedience.[21] But most of the people, within the framework of God's law and of his covenant with Israel, were free to pursue their personal dreams. They had liberty to build their lives in their own way.

It is unwise, then, to extrapolate from a few special leaders the idea that God has a fixed purpose for every Christian. While the Lord may well have a specific plan for some aspect of each person's life, mostly the divine agenda is broad enough to allow considerable flexibility.

---

[20] 1 Corinthians 9:5. Notice how Paul declares also, "Am I not free ... don't I have rights?" (vs. 1-4). Apparently he did not believe that every detail of his life was predetermined by God. I will have more to say about this later.
[21] Jeremiah 1:4-8; 20:9.

Does that seem strange, even frightening, to you? Yet there are many ways to prove not only the pliability of God's schedule, but also why nothing less could fit his larger purpose. Let us begin by showing the freedom the Lord gives you.

IN YOUR PERSONAL LIFE

Look around you, and observe the world. It is hard to see many signs of constant heavenly control. Instead, the evidence suggests divine reluctance to interfere in human affairs. Usually, the Lord prefers to let life take its ordinary course, both for the righteous and the unrighteous. Therefore the ungodly sometimes rise while godly people fall. Yet not always. Godly people often prosper, while their ungodly neighbors collapse in ruin. But you certainly cannot measure godliness by either prosperity or poverty, for both states fall upon good people and bad alike.

What we see happening around us each day, scripture also portrays. Turn for example to the book of Psalms. Listen to the laughter that ripples across its pages; but hear also the doleful sound of lament. The psalmists loved God and rejoiced in his kindness; yet they also tell their despair and voice their frustration! Anxiety often trembles in their words; anger forces itself heavenward! Search, and you will find as many Psalms of complaint as there are of praise. Dirge appears as commonly as joy. For every song that sparkles with happiness there is another that runs with tears.

What does it all mean?

Just that the ways of God were as mysterious in ancient

times as they are now! Life seemed then just as capricious and unfair as we often find it today. The Psalms show how the gamut of human hurt and happiness may as readily strike those who love God as it does those who never knew him. Pain and disappointment, heartbreak and defeat, fall impartially upon both the righteous and the unrighteous.[22]

Just a few days before writing these words I saw a newspaper report about a drunk driver. His car smashed into a busload of children who were coming home from a church camp. He killed twenty-four of them, and left many others seriously injured. What sense can anyone make of such needless deaths and such fathomless sorrow? Would anyone dare to blaspheme God by saying those children died by his express will?[23] No, when we read such things we must conclude that on the highways of life no absolute favor is shown to the righteous.[24]

ACROSS THE TRACKLESS OCEAN!

So the lesson to capture here is this: life may be just as uncertain for a believer as for an unbeliever. Today all may be going well for you; tomorrow you may be assaulted by a troop of troubles.[25] Scripture and the experience of the church alike confirm that uncertainty.

---

[22] This idea is suggested also in Matthew 5:45, which teaches that God deals impartially with everyone. Perhaps it is also valid to see in the mention of "rain" a synonym of sorrow. At least, that is its colloquial symbolism: "into each life some rain must fall."

[23] I will show later how God draws purpose out of such events, and enables us to do the same. But that is quite different from saying that he causes them, or that, in some inscrutable way, they represent his will.

[24] Except there are two things given to us that the ungodly cannot know: (1) God does sometimes choose to intervene with a miracle; (2) Christ offers a marvelous grace, more than enough to console us in the present and to carry us joyfully into his tomorrow. These things are discussed below, and in later chapters.

[25] James 4:13-16.

Which brings another lesson: if life is unsure, then we have no pledge of divine guidance strong enough to control every event. You cannot expect to hear from heaven so clearly, nor so constantly, that no shipwreck will ever overtake you. God offers no chart plain enough to navigate you around every reef. Mostly, the Father allows each day to fulfill itself in its own way; he intervenes only occasionally to change what is happening. He does step in - sometimes amazingly - but not so frequently nor so obviously as to turn life into a pathway cleared of peril.

You and I are not like trolleys, forced to run along a set of rails; rather, we are like sailing ships, with a vast ocean to move upon. Each vessel upon the sea heads toward some harbor; but there are many routes they can follow, none of them safe from the vagaries of wind and wave. Most ships do complete their voyage safely, though some must first weather fierce gales. Other vessels, however, succumb to the fury of the elements, never to be seen again.

Out there, on the turbulent ocean, does God command every storm? Does he decree a zephyr for this craft, but a hurricane for that? The ship that arrived safely, favored by calm seas and a following wind - did God ordain its smooth path? The ship that was battered into splinters and all aboard drowned - did God demand its doom? Or were both vessels merely ruled by natural and impartial laws of the sea?

Charles Dickens once sat reminiscing beside his fire, on a cold, wet night, when "the wind was blowing and sleet was driving against the dark windows." He recalled scenes from his childhood, among them the memory of a sad shipwreck -

> "See the Halsewell, East Indiaman outward bound, driving madly on a January night towards the rocks near Seacombe, on the island of Purbeck! The captain's two dear daughters are aboard, and five other ladies. The ship has been driving many hours, has seven feet of water in her hold, and her mainmast has been cut away. The description of her *loss, familiar to me from my early boyhood, seems to be read aloud as she rushes to her destiny -*
>
> *`An universal shriek, in which the voice of female distress was lamentably distinguished, announced the dreadful catastrophe. In a few moments all was hushed, except the roaring of the winds, and the dashing of the waves; the wreck was buried in the deep, and not an atom of it was ever afterwards seen.'*"[26]

How many good people have been plunged beneath the pitiless waves, to vanish for ever! Were they all drawn to that terror-filled death by some remorseless purpose of a stern Deity?

Merely to ask such questions ought to be enough to show that God infrequently alters the course of nature. Those who go down to the sea in ships place themselves at the mercy of wind and wave. They should thank God for a safe voyage; they cannot blame him for an ill one.

UPON LIFE'S UNKNOWN SEA

The same is true for the passage of life.

---

[26] My Early Times; the Folio Society, London, 1988; pg. 215.

Most Christians can expect, and will have, a peaceful and prosperous journey from earth to glory. We have a right to pray for kindly winds and a placid sea! And the voyage normally does go well for the righteous. Heaven heeds their prayers, genial skies smile upon them, good things happen to them, God bountifully supplies their *"daily bread and delivers them from evil."*[27] Christ himself strongly urged his disciples to pray about everything in life, and to expect God to meet every need generously.[28]

So we should certainly not wake in the morning with gloomy apprehensions of calamity! Let us instead greet each new day with joy, confident of the Father's favor, reaching out for his blessing, expecting a miracle, eager to see what marvelous grace his hand will bestow in the coming hours. God does care about you, he is willing to answer prayer; countless promises in scripture encourage you to seek his face boldly.

Nonetheless, life's circuit may be stormy, rent by howling gales, tossed by raging seas. Some mariners perish when the voyage is still young, their barque sunk early beneath the rampaging waves. Others carry their pilgrimage to its end, but limp into port scarred by many tempests.

So we know that sometimes the Father *does* speak to the screaming wind, forbidding it to wreak its havoc. Sometimes he *does* stretch out a mighty hand to rescue the foundering vessel.[29] Many a traveler has given thanks to God for miracles of deliverance!

---

[27] Matthew 6:9-13; Luke 11:1-5.
[28] Matthew 7:7-11; Luke 11:5-13.
[29] Psalm 107:23-32; Acts 27:13-44; plus the other two times Paul escaped drowning after a shipwreck (2 Corinthians 11:25); and, of course, the story of Jonah.

Yet, despite his poem, even the psalmist would have to admit that not every poor seaman who *"cries to the Lord in his trouble"* is *"rescued from his distress"*, nor has every beseeching prayer *"made the storm still, and hushed the heaving waves."*[30] Countless good ships have plunged into the dark depths, never to be seen again -

> Streams will not curb their pride
>   The just man not to entomb,
> Nor lightnings go aside
>   To leave his virtues room,
>   Nor is the wind less rough that
>   blows a good man's barge.
>
> Nature with equal mind
>   Sees all her sons at play,
>   Sees man control the wind,
>   The wind sweep man away;
>   Allows the proudly-riding and the
>   foundering bark.[31]

The same idea lies in Longfellow's famous poem, "The Wreck of the Hesperus" -

> It was the schooner Hesperus,
>   That sailed the wintry sea;
>   And the skipper had taken his little
>   daughter,
>   To bear him company.
>
> Blue were her eyes as the fairy-flax,
>   Her cheeks like the dawn of day,
>   And her bosom white as the

---

[30] Psalm 107:28-29.
[31] From the poem Empedocles on Etna, by Matthew Arnold (1822-1888).

> hawthorn buds,
> That ope in the month of May....

then follows an account of the dreadful storm that froze to death the captain and his crew, leaving the child alone as the ship tore towards the jagged reef....

> Then the maiden clasped her hands and
> prayed
> That saved she might be;
> And she thought of Christ, who stilled
> the wave,
> On the Lake of Galilee....

but to no avail; for the ship was driven onto the rocks by the relentless gale, and the frothing breakers pulverized it....

> At daybreak, on the bleak sea-beach,
>
> A fisherman stood aghast,
> To see the form of a maiden fair,
> Lashed close to a drifting mast.
>
> The salt sea was frozen on her breast,
> The salt tears in her eyes;
> And he saw her hair, like the brown
> seaweed,
> On the billows fall and rise....

- the poem concludes with a pious yet ironic prayer that "Christ (might) save us all from a death like this, on the reef of Norman's Woe." The child's cry did not save *her*; can I be sure that *my* plea will be any more effective?

All this is a parable of life. Sometimes the "Christ, who

stilled the wave on the Lake of Galilee" hushes the threatening gales that lash at our lives; sometimes the shipwrecked mariner is wonderfully rescued by an act of Providence; but many pilgrims, when the green waves close over their heads, must fix their last hope on heaven, not on earth.

What else can we conclude, except that divine interference in the course of a normal day is infrequent? But as soon as you say that, you destroy the idea that God has drawn a detailed map of your journey. He surely *knows* what will happen to you, but he has neither designed nor decreed your hourly path. To deny this is to make God personally responsible for every shipwreck, and that I cannot believe.

If you are still doubtful, consider this: I have heard it said that the 20th century has produced more martyrs for Christ than all previous centuries combined. At the very least, this century has been more prolific than any other in its harvest of persecution. Millions have brutally lost their lives for the sake of the gospel. What chance did *they* have for peaceful, happy, prosperous lives - murdered, raped, beaten, imprisoned, tortured, enslaved, subjected to every savagery and barbarity demon-driven minds could devise? Martyrs have to find their happiness and prosperity, their solace and peace, their treasure and satisfaction, in something deeper than material possessions and worldly success.

The same is true of those who have been struck down by some ordinary vicissitude. Life is impersonal. Scripture describes no level of divine guidance that can make us sure what tomorrow will bring – except we know this: beyond earth's tomorrow lies God's. There endless happiness dries every tear, and all sadness is erased by joy!

A BETTER PERSPECTIVE

So, like Christian in Bunyan's *Pilgrim's Progress*, we are called to stand upon the mountain-peak of faith and view a more distant horizon. The real focus of our trust must be on the shining and eternal City of God, golden and glorious in the heavens. Our destiny is the kingdom, our span is eternity, our reward is God himself. Measured against such ineffable joy, these few years on earth, with their small quotient of either pleasure or pain, are insignificant! They have in the end only one purpose: to establish our union with the Father through Christ.

I do not mean that you should passively resign yourself to wretched unhappiness, nor to unavoidable disappointment, nor to obscurity, nor to a fearful apprehension of disaster. There is nothing fatalistic about our faith. Instead, scripture strongly presumes that even in this present life believers usually fare better than unbelievers - if not materially, then certainly socially and personally. Still further, scripture expects that godliness, while it may not bring wealth, ordinarily does bring comfortable prosperity and good health. God's promises encourage us to stir up faith and to ask him for generous provision and abundant grace.[32]

Is that prayer ever denied? No, for honest faith always captures an answer and mostly the very boon it has requested. But sometimes God's answers do take a different shape than we expect. His riches do not always

---

[32] 3 John 2; Philippians 4:19; 2 Corinthians 9:8-11; and many other verses in both Old and New Testaments.

come in a form your local bank will accept! Thus his promise of health may have to await the tree of life for its true fulfillment;[33] unquenchable joy may be delayed until the sufferer stands at the Father's right hand; poverty may not be broken until the laborer's toil finds its reward in heaven. But we hold an unwavering hope in Christ: whatever we lack now in the temporal fulfillment of the promise of God will be abundantly recompensed in the ages to come.[34]

Ultimately, of course, those things are true of *every* Christian. Even the healthiest, happiest, richest, and most successful among us, when measured against heaven's standard, are sick, wretched, bankrupt, and broken! The grave swiftly eradicates all earthly distinctions, and leaves only those values that count with God -

> *"(Death) comes equally to us all, and makes us all equal when it comes. The ashes of an Oak in the Chimney, are no epitaph of that Oak, to tell me how high or how large it was. It tells me not what flocks it sheltered while it stood, nor what men it hurt when it fell. The dust of great persons' graves is speechless too; it says nothing, it distinguishes nothing. As soon the dust of a Wretch whom thou wouldest not, as of a Prince whom thou couldest not, look upon, will trouble thine eyes, if the wind blow it thither. And when a whirlwind hath blown the dust of the Churchyard into the Church, and the man sweeps out the dust of the Church into the*

---

[33] Revelation 21:4; 22:2.
[34] Compare Luke 16:25.

> *Churchyard, who will undertake to sift those dusts again, and to pronounce, This is the Patrician, this is the noble flower; and this the yeomanly, this the Plebeian bran."*[35]

So we all await the resurrection for the consummation of our hope in Christ[36]. Meanwhile, for some godly people life is a pleasant pathway through green pastures and beside still waters. But for others, it is a deep valley of bitter sorrow, constantly shadowed by pain and death, unjust, cruel, unfair. Yet what does it matter? God's sorrowing child is never alone.[37] The Father's gifts are always enough. Swiftly the moment of accomplishment will come, and in the joy of being wedded to Christ, all pain will be forgotten. Enraptured with happiness, each believing soul will taste the sweetness of the Lord for ever![38]

---

[35] John Donne (1571?-1631), English poet and divine, in a sermon preached March 8, 1622.
[36] Romans 8:18-25.
[37] 2 Corinthians 1:3-7.
[38] Romans 8:17-20; Revelation 21:4-5; 19:5-9.

Discovery

Alison's Story

WE LEARN OUR FIRST LESSONS! (1954-1955)

"Well, Ken and Alison, Ballarat needs a pastor; how would you like to go there?"

Our senior pastor paused to see what effect his words would have on us. Eagerly we nodded our heads.

"Of course. We're ready whenever you are. We'll go!"

We didn't have to pray about it, because for many months we had been asking God for an open door. The need was there, we had been looking for a place to go to, we were ready. It was as simple as that! So for three months we remained in our jobs and traveled by train seventy-five miles every weekend from Melbourne to Ballarat. After those twelve weeks, the congregation invited Ken to be their pastor, and we moved into an apartment on Main St.

Ken had studied hard to become an effective pastor, but there were still many things that only God could teach. True men of God are tutored by the Holy Spirit!

Our first year flew by. Ken took a job in a large department store, selling men's clothing to take care of our physical needs. Our eldest son, Dale, was born; Ken took his first funeral; some of our congregation moved away; others came to fill their place. By the end of the year we had gained seven members - and lost seven! We still had the grand total of twenty one members! Did we feel we had missed God's guidance? No! We were full of enthusiasm and zeal, praising God, sure that a remarkable breakthrough was coming.

In the second year, God honored our confidence. We prayed for a wife of the editor of our local newspaper, and she received an amazing healing from heart trouble. She proved to be a born evangelist, and our church began to grow.

OUR FIRST CAR

We walked one day through a local park, enjoying the warmth of a delightful summer day and the breeze dancing among the leaves of the trees. One of our favorite places was an old-fashioned glasshouse filled with exotic begonias and marvelous statuary. We arrived there, and sat on the lawn beside it, soaking up the sunshine, watching our eager little son chase the birds.

We had come there because we had a problem to discuss and to pray about. Ken was finding it increasingly difficult to fulfill all his duties as a pastor while having to rely upon public transport, or his own feet! We were wondering about the possibility of buying a car - or perhaps I should say more accurately, we were asking ourselves how we could possibly find the money to buy a car! Ken's wages did not permit such an extravagance. But perhaps we could "step out in faith" and trust God to meet the cost?

If only we could have looked into the future! This was going to be an opportunity for us to learn a vital lesson in faith and guidance. We were about to enter blindly the

Discovery

realm of presumption. Like Abraham of old we would be taught the importance of doing things God's way.

Only we didn't know that then!

"There's no doubt about it, we do need a car," I said. "It's getting difficult to visit people by bus or by walking, especially when you have to continue your work at the department store."

"Very well, we've established the need, let's pray about it and believe God for a car," said Ken decisively.

"We don't have enough money to make payments each month," I reasoned. "There's the rent, food, and clothing bills. We have a child to support now, I don't see how we can manage the extra expense."

"Just believe, Honey, that's all we have to do. We'll make the down payment, and then believe God to bring in the needed funds each month."

"Right," I agreed.

It would be such a relief to have a car, especially with the baby. Surely God didn't want us to have to walk the streets at night, wheeling our baby to meetings in the cold night air of the coming autumn? Surely he would honor our faith and somehow provide the extra money we needed?

Yes, God did want us to have a car; he even had one picked out for us, which someone would freely give us. But we didn't know that then. So we rushed in ahead of God and chose our own vehicle! It became an expensive lesson, another example of what happens when (like

Abraham) a servant of God becomes impatient and tries to force the Father's hand. Instead of "Isaac" (the child of promise), "Ishmael" is born, with sorrowful consequences.

We made the down payment, and then sat back and waited for God to increase our income by the needed amount each month. It didn't happen!

We couldn't believe it!

Slowly and painfully we came to the realization that we had gone ahead of God. This was not his way. We could not dictate to him, nor tell him how to achieve his goals, nor how to answer our prayers.

We had to face the humiliation of returning the car to the dealer, and explaining to him that we couldn't make the payments. Of course we lost our deposit, which was considerable. Then we had to confess to our church and our friends what had happened.

A few weeks later a friend who was a pastor purchased a new car, and then asked us if we would like his old one. So we had our car free of charge! It was in this little car, not very much later, that God was going to teach us another lesson about his guidance and protection.

Second Fallacy

I MUST GET GOD'S APROVAL BEFORE I DO ANYTHING

Jamie walked up to the boss and resigned from his job. When asked why, he said God had called him to be a preacher. Jamie was a good worker, and his employer was sorry to lose him. "Any time you want a job," he said, "come and see me. There'll be one waiting for you." Only two weeks later Jamie was back, asking for his old position again. The boss was puzzled. "Why have you returned so soon? What happened to your call to the ministry?" The young man replied: *"After hearing me preach the last two Sundays, God changed his mind!"*[39]

Do you smile? Yet that story is all too close to the experience of many people. Yesterday they were sure God had spoken. Today they have changed their minds, only to get a still different word from heaven tomorrow. Is the Lord really so capricious? More likely such people are confusing their personal whim with the divine voice.

But the problem remains: how can you tell if God is speaking to you? What is the difference between a prompting from the Holy Spirit and a mere fancy of your own spirit? Should you ever expect to hear from God?

Beyond question, the Father does speak to his children; the Lord does give personal instruction to his servants. It

---

[39] Unhappily, I have forgotten who told me this joke.

would be hard to imagine a Christian who *never* hears from God, never gets any direction from heaven. Nonetheless, I hope you are not like those people who insist on receiving divine guidance for almost everything in their daily lives. They refuse to do *anything* until they first get a "word" from God. I have met Christians who deem a heavenly "all-clear" essential before they so much as step outside their homes. I once visited a family where even a decision to make a prosaic phone call had to be preceded by falling on our knees to pray for God's permission!

Inescapably, people who surrender to such magical piety become as superstitious as a pagan witchdoctor. They see omens in a thousand frivolous ways and places: passing cats and missed trains; thunder storms and soft zephyrs; someone home or absent; inner feelings or the lack of them; a telephone ring or silence - all are read as augurs of the divine will. I know a pastor who can see the ominous hand of God in a piece of paper rustling along a footpath! I hope you have not become prey to such fantasies.

But surely there are *some* things it is risky to attempt before hearing from God? When is it safe to go ahead? When must I wait until the Lord speaks?

A good place to begin is scripture. Whatever stands there already disapproved, remains disapproved, and must be banished from Christian conduct. Whatever stands there already approved, remains approved, and should be welcomed immediately.

Thus the premise, *"get God's approval before doing anything,"* is obviously true in the sense of not doing anything you know God *disapproves*. But it is not true in the sense of expecting that you can or should get a *"word"* from God about every matter. There is a spurious piety, and an even more spurious supernaturalism, in that attitude.

Do you think that is too harsh? Perhaps the following ideas will change your mind!

A SILENT HEAVEN

We are all prone to be frustrated by the long silences of God, and the seeming lack of divine activity. We can't understand why the Lord doesn't work more vigorously, or at least more visibly. We know what *we* would do if *we* had limitless power! Quickly, sinners would be called to order. Swiftly, iniquity would be punished and righteousness rewarded. The entire planet would be at once obliged to behave itself! Some of us even feel like Martin Luther, who is reputed to have said: *"If I were God, and the world treated me like it has treated him, I would kick the wretched thing to pieces!"* God's patience seems not only limitless but also inexplicable. His silence disturbs us, for we are restless activists; inertia makes us anxious; so we cry out with the prophet -

> *"Why don't' you rend the heavens and come down upon us? Why don't you crumble the mountains in to dust? Oh, that you would start a fire! Then, like brushwood set ablaze, like water boiling out of a pot, your enemies would flee from your name, and the nations would hide from your coming. Oh, that you would do sudden miracles, such as we have*

> *never seen before! Then every great mountain would surely collapse before you!"*[40]

Ordinarily those spectacular displays of power are the very things God will not do. He prefers Bethlehem to Sinai, the hidden mystery of the incarnation to blazing skies and toppling mountains. Jesus understood this heart of the Father, therefore he rebuked the "sons of thunder" when they wanted to call down lightning bolts from heaven.[41]

Thirty centuries ago, Elijah learned the same lesson- although we are still reluctant to hear it. The Lord prefers, not the strong wind, nor the rumbling earthquake, nor the consuming flame, but *"the still, small, voice"*.[42] The apostle taught the same, although we remain disappointed with his dictum -

> *"For God has not brought you to things that may be touched, to a blazing fire, to gloomy pitch blackness, to a raging storm and blaring trumpet, to a voice speaking such words that the listeners begged to hear no more...Rather, you have come to Mount Zion, and to the City of the living God, the heavenly Jerusalem, along with a vast company of gaily appareled angels, to the gathering of the first-born who are enrolled in heaven."*[43]

We love the second part of that scene - heavenly, spiritual, transcendent - but we do wish God had not altogether

---

[40] Isaiah 64:1-3.
[41] Luke 9:54-55.
[42] 1 Kings 19:11-13.
[43] Hebrews 12:18-23.

abandoned the first! We feel that so many problems could be instantly solved, so many pains healed, if only the Lord would once again rip open the sky and show some of that old-time power! Just a couple of fiery explosions, Lord! Just a brief appearance by a burning archangel, tall as the clouds, brandishing a flaming sword! Then the people would surely flock to church, and sinners would abandon their wicked ways!

That is not the way of the Lord. The poet, copying the prophet, had a better understanding –

> "Breathe through the heats of our desire
> Thy coolness and thy balm;
> Let sense be dumb, let flesh retire,
> Speak through the earthquake, wind, and fire,
> O still, small voice of calm!"[44]

One day, of course, on the last day, God *will* act with awful majesty and visible glory.[45] But this is a day of grace, a time during which the Father is seeking, not terrified slaves, but willing and loving children. This is an hour of persuasion, not of power, a season when those are specially blessed who, though they have *not* seen, yet believe.[46]

Thus we have to learn to live with seeming silence, to walk by faith, not by sight.[47] God *is* speaking and acting, every moment of every day,[48] but in ways that are more often hidden than overt, affecting our inner spirits rather

---

[44] From the hymn, Dear Lord and Father of Mankind, by John Greenleaf Whittier; 1872.
[45] Matthew 26:64; 2 Thessalonians 1:6-10; Revelation 6:12-17; and many other references.
[46] John 20:29.
[47] 2 Corinthians 5:7.
[48] John 5:17.

than our conscious minds. We see his hand in the past more than we recognize it in the present. As we look back, we realize how the Lord has gently yet effectively guided our steps, bringing about his own good purpose. Gradually, we come to understand that we hear and obey mostly without being aware of it!

None of this means that God *never* speaks openly, or that he *never* acts overtly. Countless Christians, now and in the past, have heard the voice of the Lord, and they have seen his hand mightily at work. Let Paul stand for them all: consider his extraordinary conversion on the road to Damascus, the earthquake that released him from jail at Philippi, his transport into the third heaven, and the like. Paul had visions and revelations it was unlawful for him to share with any other person. But was that his daily experience? No, even for that amazing man, such events were uncommon. Most days for Paul were like they are for us: heaven resolutely silent; the Father apparently a spectator; no visible divine aid available.[49]

ASK FOR WISDOM

Perhaps you are protesting: *"What about the instruction James gives, to pray for wisdom when you lack it? Surely we are encouraged there to expect a word from heaven?"* [50]

That depends upon how you understand *"wisdom"*. The Greeks had two different words, both of which were connected with wisdom: *sophia*, and *gnosis*. The first was used to describe an inner, intuitive, understanding; the second related more to external knowledge. James used

---

[49] See Chapters Four & Six below, for a more detailed study of Paul's approach to divine guidance. James 1:5.
[50] James 1:5

Discovery

the first. He said we should pray for *sophia*. Is that important? Yes, because it reaches beyond asking God for occasional guidance; it seeks a higher level, where you instinctively know what the Lord wants - not in the sense of ticking off a list of specific instructions; but through an innate awareness of his purpose. What the Father disapproves, you intuitively shun; what the Father approves, you naturally embrace.

Sophia describes an insight into the true nature of things. It is distinct from merely practical decisions about conduct. It is the wisdom that enables one to make the right choice without any external help. Those who possess *sophia* effortlessly select the path approved by God; the mind of Christ has already been developed within them. Admittedly, no one can reach this state in a day. *Sophia* is not a momentary acquisition. It is wisdom born out of much prayer, wrought by study and by growth in grace.

The difference between *sophia* and *gnosis* can be illustrated in several ways:

contrast a trained motor engineer, who understands the inner dynamics of an internal combustion engine, with a beginner driver who needs a driver's manual. The manual represents *gnosis*, which the learner has to depend upon to get some use out of his vehicle. But the deeper knowledge possessed by the engineer is *sophia*. If the vehicle breaks down, the novice must call for help, while the engineer does his own repairs. Not only that, the engineer knows how to modify his car, altering its shape or its mechanical structure. His *sophia* gives him extensive control over its performance and style. He is independent of, he scorns for his personal use, the *gnosis* found in a new-owner's manual.

-or, look at a young boy who must begin by closely following the pattern book included with his construction set. Later, he will abandon the book, and design his own cranes, cars, ships, and other toys. What has happened? He has gone from *gnosis* (an external knowledge) to *sophia* (an inner sense of how to use the bits and pieces of his set.) How disappointed his father would be if the boy never graduated beyond the book of simple examples! How proud the son makes his father when he produces his first original model! It is natural for children to break loose from restraint, and to express their creative energies. They yearn to advance beyond *gnosis* to *sophia*. They struggle to deserve and to get ever greater independence from the guiding hands of the adult world around them.

Remember the Bible is one story, one history, His story, the story of Jesus Christ. All through the ages we find the promise of a Savior. (Luke 19:10)
(Matthew 20:28)

BABES OR ADULTS?

Unhappily, many Christians prefer to stay toddlers, always wanting or needing every decision to be made for them by God. Such clinging dependence, when we are taking our first hesitant steps in Christ, surely delights the Father. But it must grieve him to find his children years later still clutching his hand![51]

When each of my four children were tiny, and had just learned to walk, it was my proud joy to put a harness and leash on them, and take them shopping. I would hardly

---

[51] Think about Hebrews 5:11-6:3; and other similar passages.

like to do so now, when they are all adults! How ashamed I would be if you saw one of my grown sons running on ahead of me, straining on a tether like an unruly baby!

The eager goal of parents, beginning with severance of the umbilical cord, is to nurture their children so that one by one each restraint can be cast off. The task is done when the child can be trusted with adult responsibility. Then the final string is loosed, and the former infant goes out into the world alone. The parents are not anxious. They have instilled high standards and a noble character into their offspring. They know their son or daughter will do what is right without having to call father or mother every day.

Alison and I have been married (as of this writing) nearly 40 years. On our wedding day, she was 19 and I was 20 - hardly more than children! Yet our respective parents knew they had done their work well. So they sent us off, never doubting that our lives would reflect the virtues they had built into us. Fear that we might disgrace their good names was scornfully rejected. They trusted us to do as they would do themselves. They hoped we would do even better![52]

Our heavenly Father surely wants to establish the same kind of relationship with *his* spiritual offspring. Not a bond of infant dependence and helplessness; but one that reflects are increasing maturity in Christ. He seeks, not more, but less direct control over our lives. What could

---

[52] Proverbs 22:6. The promise of this scripture is not infallible. The Bible itself contains many examples of children nurtured in the Lord who went astray. No parent has any absolute guarantee that a son or daughter will not break their heart. Nonetheless, there remains a very strong presumption that children will not depart from a good character, if that character is firmly instilled into them.

please him better than to recognize in you and me someone he can trust to behave honorably and wisely? What could disappoint him more than a child who refuses to grow up, one who should be adult but must still be spoon-fed and diapered? Yet some Christians suppose they will reach the pinnacle of spiritual attainment only when God does all their thinking for them, and makes all their decisions! They prefer mental and spiritual vacuity to a mature and responsible walk with the Father. They choose to remain babies rather than become his grown-up (or at least growing-up) children. It is an attitude that seems to me strangely perverse, contrary to life and to God's normal pattern.

A general, who has trained his field commanders well, needs to give them only a broad outline of his plan. He can send them off to war, trusting each captain to make sound tactical decisions within the parameters of his strategy. He knows they will not act against the larger battle-plan he has laid before them. He is confident that every maneuver they employ will hasten the victory of the whole army.

Likewise, the Captain of our Faith, mobilizing *his* forces for war, should not have to give detailed instructions to every soldier - not even to those who are high in his command. It is enough that we know his larger resolve, and that he is building into us his own character. Surely he can trust us more and more to act correctly without any immediate input from him?

Ten centuries before Christ, Solomon grasped this lesson. It is time for us to learn it too! The wise king said -

> *"Common sense comes from the Lord, and by his words you will learn knowledge and wisdom...Then you will readily tell right from wrong, maintaining good balance in every decision, always choosing the correct path. Therefore, allow his knowledge to enter your mind, penetrating to the roots of your soul; then you will experience deep joy...Discretion will become your guardian, and wisdom will be your protection...The pathway of a good man will naturally become your own. Almost without trying, you will follow the ways of the righteous!"*[53]

DIMINISHING GUIDANCE

Here then is a discovery that surprises many devout Christians: advancing spiritual maturity brings not clearer guidance or more dependence upon God for daily instruction, but a diminishing need for both of them!

> *"It might be thought by those who have not found themselves in a position of leadership that greater experience and a longer walk with God would result in much greater ease in discerning the will of God in perplexing situations. But the reverse is often the case. God treats the leader as a mature adult, leaving more and more to his spiritual discernment, and giving fewer sensible and tangible evidences of his guidance than in earlier years. This perplexity adds to the inevitable pressures incidental to any*

---
[53] Proverbs 2:6-20

> *responsible office."*
>
> "In one of his few moments of self-revelation, D. E. Hoste said to a friend:
>
> *' ... I more and more see that as we go on in the Christian life, the Lord very often does not want to give us the sense of his presence, or the consciousness of his help. There again Mr. Hudson Taylor helped me very much. We were talking about guidance. He said how in his younger days, things used to come so clearly, so quickly to him. "But," he said, "now as I have gone on, and God has used me more and more, I seem often to be like a man going along in a fog. I do not know what to do."'*
>
> *"But when the time came to act, God always responded to his servant's trust."*[54]

The immortal Bach faced the same dilemma. His melodies may well outlast the earthly church, bringing joy for ever even to the gathered angels in heaven. His glorious gift gave him as much claim to divine inspiration as any man who ever lived. Yet he too, as his biography shows, lamented the difficulties he encountered when he tried to discern the will of God.

He was not alone. It is simply true, as the quotation above declares; many of the noblest and finest of God's servants have wrestled with this quandary. There are few (if any) great spiritual leaders who have claimed the constant and supernatural guidance some people endlessly crave. Most

---

[54] J. Oswald Sanders, Spiritual Leadership; Lakeland, 1970; pg. 112,113

of the men and women who have wrought mightily for the Lord have had to do so in the midst of mystery and uncertainty. God's strength is made perfect through our weakness.

GUIDANCE IS POSSIBLE

Does this mean you should stop praying for guidance? Of course not. Every day you should submit your mind, your spirit, your life to the Father's control; you should always be open to receive divine counsel, including specific (and even supernatural) instruction. Always be ready for the Spirit to invade your life! Tell the Lord he is welcome to take charge of your affairs, to turn you in another direction, to reshape your plans!

Isaiah angrily denounced those "obstinate children" who, stubbornly ignoring God's wishes, refused to consult the Lord, rebuffed the Holy Spirit, and rushed to form their own "alliance".[55] God always reserves the right - as he did with Joshua - to tell his servants "when to go out and when to come in". Nothing but trouble ever befell Israel when the people failed "to enquire of the Lord".[56]

God has spoken in the past, he still speaks today, and he will surely continue to speak tomorrow. So remain alert every day for the voice of the Lord! Be ready for the intervening hand of God! Welcome with joy any interruption from heaven!

Yet tension remains between passages like those above, which urge dependence upon God, and others that place strong emphasis on careful thought, and responsible

---
[55] 30:1-2.
[56] Malachi 3:6; Hebrews 13:8; James 1:17.

planning. Should pre-eminence be given to prayer, or to pragmatism?

No doubt we show the highest wisdom when we reach an easy balance between the two, a state of spiritual equilibrium that enables us to choose correctly whether to act on personal initiative or to seek special direction from God. Both forms of decision making have a valid function in the Spirit-led life. See, for example, Acts 8:26-28, *where an angel guided Philip supernaturally into the desert; but the Ethiopian was guided unaware, both in his journey and in his reading of Isaiah. If you are walking in harmony with the Lord, you too will know both of those experiences: sometimes guidance will come to you consciously; sometimes unperceived.*

Again, on some matters you will absolutely need a clear "word" from God; and even if you do not really need one, the Lord may be willing to give it to you. The Father is not averse to gladdening his children with serendipities of revelation. Yet on other matters, whether you "need" a word or not, heaven may remain silent. Perhaps God wants you to develop maturity by deciding for yourself what to do, when to do it, and how.

It may sometimes happen that your need for a heavenly word is so imperative that you dare not move until God speaks. Then wait, no matter how painful the waiting, until you receive the Commander's orders. But such times will be infrequent. Ordinarily it is foolish to wait indefinitely for a miracle of guidance. The occasions are rare when you could offend God by acting in good faith, even if the decision you make proves to have been wrong. Right or wrong, if you have acted honorably and sincerely, the Lord will work with gracious might to fashion your deeds to his glory and your reward.

DIVINE UNPREDICTABILITY

From one viewpoint God is forever the same, he never changes.[57] This is especially true of his moral character, his eternal promise, and the like. But in other ways (as we have seen) the Lord is marvelously unpredictable, delighting in doing the unforeseen. Hence the familiar saying is only partly true: "what he has done for others he will do for you." It is more correct to say that the Lord deals differently with each of his children, based on the diverse needs they all have.

A dramatic demonstration of this principle can be found in Matthew 14, which begins with the ugly story of John's murder. The prophet sat bleakly alone in his cell, seemingly abandoned even by God, until, at the cruel and unjust behest of a hateful woman, he was foully beheaded. Where was Jesus? He didn't even visit John in prison - yet nothing could have stopped him from doing so had he chosen to. John was Jesus' cousin, and so had a double claim upon his support. Instead, Christ and his disciples put as much water as they could between themselves and Herod, and found refuge on the other side of the lake, in the desert.

You might think that Jesus didn't care, or perhaps after all had no power to help, except that suddenly the story transports us to a beautiful and peaceful afternoon, near Galilee. An immense crowd is sitting on the grassy shore, listening eagerly as Jesus taught them about the kingdom

---

[57] Malachi 3:6; Hebrews 13:8; James 1:17

of God. He looks at them with compassion and heals their sick; and in the evening, noticing their hunger, he graciously feeds them by a miracle. They had neither asked for nor expected such an astonishing gift. Nor had they or the disciples the slightest faith for such a miracle. It was simply a spontaneous kindness by Jesus. But why such sympathy for the fickle crowd when seemingly there was none for John? They enjoyed a supernatural banquet on a pleasant hillside, while the butchered prophet lay in his own blood, forsaken on the dungeon floor.

Suddenly the scene changes again. Now we are out on Galilee facing disaster under the battering of a fierce storm. Jesus advances toward the boat, walking on the sea. He calls Peter to come to him, a challenge to faith. The big fisherman rises to the challenge, jumps out of the boat and begins to walk across the heaving waves. Suddenly the realization of what he is doing, and where he is, overwhelms him, and he begins to sink. But Jesus stretches out his hand, rescues Peter, escorts him across the water to the boat, and hushes the storm. Here is a mixture of bold faith (for Peter did *walk on the water) and of divine initiative.*

When Jesus and the disciples arrive at the other side of the lake, the people rush to him, clamoring to touch even the fringe of his robe, and everyone who touches him is at once made whole. The picture here is one of Jesus responding to eager desire for a miracle.

How diverse those scenes are! How differently each group of people is treated! John appears to be forsaken, trembling in his bleak cell; unpitied and unheeded, waiting alone for a violent death; yet for the crowd on the sunny slope there is gentle compassion and a miracle of supply. From Peter a high level of faith is demanded; yet Jesus responded willingly to the shaky and variable trust of the pressing multitude.

Thus Matthew shows us that sometimes the Lord acts only in response to great faith; while at other times, he yields to little or no faith. Sometimes he intervenes with gracious miracles of supply and extraordinary rescue; other times he leaves his despairing child shivering in a frightful cell waiting for an unknown fate.

Each new setting brings a different action from heaven, a different gift, a different demand. That is the way of the Lord. You cannot straitjacket him into a rigidly identical approach to all his servants. For one he does this thing, for another that. From one he demands an enormous sacrifice, from another hardly anything. One is led beside still waters, another through the cold, dark valley. To one he gives one kind of bounty, to another a different kind. For one there is a mighty demonstration of divine power; for another heaven remains silent, and the hand of God still.[58]

---

[58] Just this morning I read the story of Sir Bors in Sir Thomas Malory's legend of Camelot (written 500 years ago). Sir Bors was in quest of the Holy Grail, but he offended his brother Sir Lionel, who challenged him to mortal combat. Sir Bors refused to fight with his own brother, and he was struck to the ground by Sir Lionel, and sore wounded. At that moment a holy hermit came running to them and threw himself over Sir Bors, to protect him. Despite Sir Lionel's threats, the priest Continued from page 42...refused to move, so his head was cut from his shoulders. Sir Lionel then lifted his sword again against his brother, only to be stopped by another knight, Sir Colgrevaunce. They two fell into combat, and Sir Colgrevaunce was slain. Once more Sir Lionel turned toward Sir Bors, who at last reluctantly drew his own sword to defend himself. But first he prayed: "May God show his miracle upon us both; now God have mercy upon me, though I defend my life against my brother." Whereupon a voice spoke from heaven, "Flee, Sir Bors, and touch him not, or else thou shalt slay him." And then "a cloud alighted between them in the likeness of a fire with a marvelous flame, so that both their two shields burned." This miracle caused a reconciliation between the brothers, and Sir

When Peter asked Jesus, "Lord, about this man?" the master said to him. "If is my will that he should remain until I come, what is that to you? You just follow me!"[59]

What is it to you if the Lord leads his servants along different paths, and deals with them in different ways? We ought not to be envious of each other, nor arrogate to the will of God as we each see it, submissive in our hearts, trusting in our minds, sure that the Father will fulfill through us all that he has purposed

---

Bors went on to become one of the three knights who alone were permitted to look upon the Grail. A silent question lies over the story: why did God work a miracle to rescue Sir Bors and Sir Lionel (who ill deserved it), but suffered the brave priest and the courteous knight to perish. Malory had the good sense to leave that moral problem unresolved. He knew too much about life to try to reduce it to a rule of fairness. Life is not fair. The ways of God remain mysterious. (Le Morte D'Arthur, edited by R. M. Lumiansky; Collier Books, New York, 1982; Part VI.6.9-12.)

[59] John 21:21-22.

Alison's Story

SAVED BY ANGELS! (1956)

How marvelous it was to have a vehicle at last! We thanked God from our hearts for the Father's kind provision. Our lesson learned, we threw ourselves with renewed vigor into the work of the church. By winter we were ready for a vacation. We decided to visit our parents in Adelaide, 400 miles away.

We drove out of Ballarat along a magnificent memorial avenue of trees, planted by the relatives of soldiers killed during the war. Our conversation as we began the journey was again about the puzzling aspects of divine guidance.

"Ken, how can we be sure that we are in the will of God? How can we know that this trip is his will? Does he expect us to ask him about every little thing, or should we just live our lives normally, and only ask his guidance for specific things?"

"I asked an older pastor about that very thing recently," Ken began, "and he gave me an answer I'll never forget. It's like this. You should first pray and ask for God's guidance, and then simply *believe* that he has heard your prayer. After that, it becomes *God's* task to make sure you are in his will."

"But what if you aren't in his will," I queried.

"Then he will maneuver circumstances until you *are* in his will. Don't you see? So long as you trust God, the obligation is no longer yours, but his."

Slowly I began to relax as we sped through the vast Australian countryside. I thanked God for another lesson learned. It was so simple. A concept that would stand us in good stead in the years to come. No more agonizing over whether we were in the will of God, just a simple prayer of faith -

"Father, we want to be in the centre of your will. So from now on we will simply trust that we are there. We know that you will then honor our faith and arrange circumstances to ensure that we do not deviate from your path for us. Amen."

I cuddled my little son in my arms and drifted off to sleep, secure in the knowledge that God himself was watching over us. He was in control of our lives and he would guide and direct us, shaping at least the *outcome* of each event, if not the event itself.

I didn't know it then, but it would not be very long before we would have a terrifying opportunity to experience this very protection.

A few days after arriving in Adelaide and sharing a joyful reunion with our families, we decided to take a trip to Victor Harbor. This is a beautiful part of the South Australian shoreline, and a popular picnic spot.

We expected a time of refreshing in body and spirit.

The air was chilly, but the sky was blue, the sun was brightly shining, and it was a perfect day for a country drive. So we motored through the hills, reveling in the glorious views stretched out before us.

The time together at the beach was everything we had hoped for, and when we finally packed up to return home we were weary but rejuvenated. It had been delightful to play with our baby son on the beautiful white sands, and to paddle with him in the salt water.

As we traveled through the twisting winding hills on our return journey we noticed a sign on the side of the road, "STEEP INCLINE AROUND NEXT BEND." Naturally, we expected to find a sharply rising hill after the next turn in the road. So Ken accelerated to accommodate the slope. Alas, instead of an upgrade we found to our horror that we were plunging down a steep *decline* (not an *incline*). Our car only had mechanical brakes, and when the drums were hot after a long trip, as they were now, they did not function very well.

It all happened so quickly. Afterward Ken told me he was sure we were going to die. He remembers distinctly crying out, "Lord, here we come!"

We were traveling too fast. We were gaining speed. The brakes were ineffective, and we could not make the next corner. Instead we would be hurtled into space to smash onto the valley floor far below.

But God had not finished with us yet! He had other plans for us. Just as the car was about to go over the edge it stopped! Just like that! We sat there, shaken but alive, praising God for deliverance from a terrible death.

There was absolutely no natural reason why our car should have halted on the edge of that cliff. We could only suppose God had intervened in that moment - perhaps by an angel - to arrest the vehicle. There was no slowing down. One moment we were traveling at high speed, and the next we had come to an abrupt halt - yet we were not jolted or hurt in the slightest.

We backed up slowly and then, with trembling but thankful hearts, traveled the remainder of our way home. How grateful we were to the Lord for this sign that we were indeed in his will and under his protection!

A week later we were to experience yet another instance of God's tender care.

We were traveling back to Ballarat through the Adelaide Hills, and looking forward to another year of fruitful work for the Lord. Suddenly we saw a car wheel roll past us on the left. It trundled to a stop and leaned crazily against the fence on the side of the road.

Meanwhile our car lurched, and we realized with a shock that we had been watching one of our own back wheels! Ken quickly stopped the car and we tumbled out to assess the damage.

"Thank God it was the back wheel," Ken exclaimed. "Had it been a front wheel we could have been killed or been the cause of a terrible accident."

We were so young and inexperienced! Did we have any tools, or even a jack? We began to look.

Just then two policemen in a car pulled up beside *us.* They had seen the whole thing and had stopped to help us.

"Do you have any tools?" they asked.

Discovery

With some embarrassment Ken had to reply, "Well, you see officer, this is our first car, and we aren't very well equipped yet."

"Let me help," laughed the policeman. He got out his wheel jack and tools, and in no time had our wheel back on. Then he gave us a lesson in mechanics. He tightened the nuts on all the other wheels, while patiently explaining that it is a good idea, before starting on a long journey, to check your wheels - especially on a car built in 1938!

Feeling little foolish, we thanked the two officers heartily, and continued on our way. We praised God that a rear wheel, and not one of our front ones, had come off first. We thanked God also for an understanding policeman with a sense of humor.

'I wonder, did you arrange to have him ride behind us Lord, or was it just a coincidence?"

Third Fallacy

I CAN TEST THE WILL OF GOD WITH A 'FLEECE'

For seven years, at harvest time, bandits had ravaged the farmland, stealing the wheat and corn, burning what they could not steal, driving off the livestock, and enslaving anybody they could catch. Against these marauders the terrified people were helpless. So they hid themselves in caves and deep valleys, high in the mountains, or in the few strongholds that remained. Impoverished, cowering, defenseless, they cried out to God.

An angel suddenly stood before a young farmer, who was anxiously threshing a little wheat in a winepress, hoping no enemy would spot him. *"The Lord is with you, mighty warrior!"* the angel began, and then told him to raise an army and liberate the oppressed nation.

The young man listened with astonishment. What did he, born to hold a plough, know about battle? His hands were trained to wield an ox-goad, not a sword. How could he forge a rabble of dispirited civilians into an invincible fighting force?

But the heavenly messenger was adamant: by this farmer, and him alone, the Lord had resolved to rescue the people.

Who was this reluctant hero? You have recognized him already: Gideon, whose story is told in Judges 6:36-8:32.

Gideon's adventures were many, and his exploits marvelous; but probably he stands most renowned as the man who tested the will of God by using a fleece. One night he spread out some wool on a threshing floor, saying to God, *"Let the morning dew form only on the fleece, while the surrounding ground remains dry."* So it happened; but he was not satisfied. The next evening he said again, *"Tonight let the fleece remain dry, while dew covers the ground."* And again his request was granted.

This time Gideon was content, and he blew the trumpet, gathered an army, and marched off to drive the Mideanites out of Israel.

USING A "FLEECE"

Many Christians have found in the story of Gideon a license to put out a "fleece", that is, some test or other to find the will of God. Their test, like Gideon's, usually depends upon whether or not a particular event happens: a telephone call; somebody's arrival; receiving a sum of money; a letter; and the like.

How reliable is this? Is it a mark of maturity? How willing is God to respond to a "fleece"?

Asking for such "signs" from God is not commended in scripture. Heaven's frown, more than divine favor, is likely to rest upon those who crave these "proofs" of God's activity.[60]

---
[60] Matthew 12:39; etc.

Across the entire span of Biblical history, no-one apart from Gideon ever used this woolly device to catch a word from God. Some others did employ similar stratagems - for example Moses[61], and Hezekiah[62] - but the context usually shows that their demand for a sign was a mark, not of faith, but of unbelief. Though God yielded to it, he was displeased. The result - as in Hezekiah's case - was often negative.

So it was with Gideon. The low level of spirituality shown by his fleeces led to his ultimate downfall[63]. Scripture admires Gideon for his heroism and obedience; but his poor spiritual discernment is hardly something for Christians to emulate! Follow rather the example of Christ. Can you imagine Jesus using a piece of wet wool to learn the will of his Father?[64]

God may, and does, deal with each of us on the level of our present understanding and need, and of our growth in grace. But that is no excuse for clinging to recognized immaturity. Let us be done with childish ways, and begin to show ourselves full-grown in Christ.[65] We are possessors of the Holy Spirit; we should aim to have the mind of Christ.[66]

UNRELIABLE OMENS

Fleece hunters, omen readers, dream seekers, are prone to hear what they want to hear, sometimes unconsciously.

---

[61] Exodus 4:1, ff.
[62] 2 Kings 20:8-18.
[63] If you have not yet done so, read the sad story of his declining years, especially Judges 8:24-27.
[64] I have a feeling that this saying is not one of my inventions, but that I heard it used somewhere, coined by another.
[65] 1 Corinthians 13:11; Ephesians 4:13; Hebrews 5:11-6:3.
[66] 1 John 2:27-28; 1 Corinthians 2:16.

Thus Jeremiah once encountered some people who were eager for a word from God - but only while the Lord said what they wanted to hear.

Jeremiah warned them about the dire consequences of pressing their will against God's command. They refused to listen, and ruin overtook them.[67]

Their imitators are many. Determined to put words into God's mouth, these foolish people keep seeking a sign or an omen until one arrives that confirms their desire. This superstitious hunger for a divine augur is antagonistic to mature and responsible faith. Any kind of fetishism ought to be repugnant to us. Let us rather agree with Paul, and grow up, and put away childish things, remaining "babes" only in evil, but otherwise showing maturity in our thinking.[68] Those who reject this, who insist on indulging their illusions, leave the way open for satanic deception. They should heed Sirach's earnest warning -

> *"People who abandon good sense will be led astray by empty hope; and a simpleton allows a mere dream to give wings to his folly. Try catching a shadow; try chasing the wind – you will have better success than those who take notice of dreams! What is a dream? Just a reflection, like the mirror-image of your own face, which though you see it, lacks substance. Does this dream not come from your own mind? How then can it be pure! Does it not come from you won heart? Why then do you trust it!*

---

[67] Jeremiah 42:2-22.
[68] 1 Corinthians 13:11; 14:20.

> *"Divinations, omens, dreams – they are all empty fantasies...Sometimes, it is true, dreams may come from the Most High; but mostly you should pay no attention to them. Too many dreamers have been pulled into error by their vision! The law is complete by itself; such fantasies can add nothing to it."*[69]

"Divinations, omens, and dreams," said Sirach, "are all an illusion. The things you already want to see or hear, those are what your mind conjures up!" How often I have observed that folly over the years. Be warned! It is easy to be deluded! Don't rush to accept every dream, vision, or voice that presents itself as a messenger from heaven. Perhaps it is; but more likely it is not!

The unknown author of the "Didache" gave the same warning to Christians early in the second century -

> *"Do not always be looking for omens, my son, for this leads to idolatry. Likewise, have nothing to do with witchcraft, astrology or magic; do not even consent to be a witness of such practices, for they too can all breed idolatry...*
>
> *"Accept as good whatever experience comes your way, in the knowledge that nothing can happen without God."*[70]

Athanasius tells us the amazing story of St. Anthony, a famous "desert saint" of the 3rd century. In a celebrated

---

[69] Sirach 34:1-8.
[70] Didache I.3; tr. by Maxwell Staniforth; Early Christian Writings, Penguin Books, 1968; pg. 228-229.

passage on demons, Anthony warns against being gullibly misled by a hunger for supernatural guidance

> *"Wherefore there is no need to set much value on these things, nor for the sake of them to practice a life of discipline and labor; but that living well we may please God. And we neither ought to pray to know the future, nor to ask for it as the reward of our discipline; but our prayer should be that the Lord may be our fellow-helper for victory over the devil...*
>
> "When therefore they (seducing spirits/ dreams/visions) come by night to you and wish to tell the future, or say, `we are the angels,' give no heed, for they lie ... (A true vision from the angels) comes so quietly and gently that immediately joy, gladness, and courage arise in the soul ... (and) the thoughts of the soul remain unruffled and undisturbed...."[71]

A millennium later, in one of his famous Canterbury Tales, Geoffrey Chaucer sang the same refrain. He tells the story of King Croesus, the fabulously wealthy monarch of Lydia.[72] The Persian emperor Cyrus had condemned Croesus to be burned to death, but a sudden shower of rain extinguished the flames. Everyone interpreted the unexpected downpour as a sign of heaven's favor, so Cyrus released Croesus and sent him home with many gifts.

Vaunting pride then gripped him, and he began to

---

[71] The Nicene and Post-Nicene Fathers: Second Series; Vol. Four; "Athanasius"; Eerdmans Publishing Company reprint; 1978; pg 205 ("Life of St Anthony," 35,36).

[72] The original story is found in the histories of Herodotus (I.86-88), and is probably true in its general outline.

contemplate another bold attack upon the mighty Persian Empire. Would heaven prosper the enterprise, he wondered? Soon he slept and dreamed, and awoke certain that the gods would make him triumphant. In his slumber

> He dreamt that he was
> perching in a tree,
> With Jupiter to wash him,
> back and side,
> While Phoebus, with a towel
> fair to see,
> Was drying him.
> This was what swelled his pride.

He told the dream to his daughter, who warned him that it might not mean what it appeared to say. But her royal father brushed aside her caution and launched his attack. The Persians routed his army, and this time no merciful deity intervened to save Croesus from their fierce vengeance. Thus the prophecy was fulfilled: he was "perched in a tree" *(hanged as a rebel);* "Jupiter washed him back and side" *(with rain and snow as he swung on the gibbet); and* "Phoebus dried him with a fair towel" *(the warm sun and gentle breezes played around his swaying corpse).*

Thus the trickery of dreams! Hence Chaucer said -

> Dreams are a vanity, God knows, pure error.
> Dreams are engendered in
> the too-replete
> From vapors in the belly,
> which compete

With others, too abundant, swollen tight ....[73]

So beware of dreams! Many have followed them to destruction. Few have found in them a beacon to the purpose of God.

PROMISE BOXES

Another kind of commonly used "fleece" is the ubiquitous "Promise Box" - those nicely presented collections of pleasant Bible verses, printed on little scrolls of paper. They occupy a cheerful place on a mantelpiece, and are useful when you feel like enjoying a morsel of spiritual candy. You risk no discomfort, for it is unthinkable that the box will contain any harsh message! So with easy conscience, like plucking toffee out of a jar, you can choose a random scroll and savor the sweet words it contains.

No harm exists in a "Promise Box" until some foolish person begins to depend upon it for daily guidance. Then it becomes perilous indeed. If I had not seen it with my own eyes I could hardly believe that people would trust such a childish way to find the mind of God. Could there be a shallower, or less satisfactory, or more flippant method of sustaining spiritual life? How far removed this is from the serious duty we all have to "*let the word of Christ dwell in us richly*".[74]

Because his people often allow him no other way, God must sometimes speak to them by inadequate means, even through the worst kinds of Biblical hocus pocus; but that does not excuse immaturity. We should aim to grow up!

---

[73] The Canterbury Tales, by Geoffrey Chaucer; tr. Nevill Coghill; Penguin Classics; 1977. From "The Monk's Tale" (pg 229,230); and "The Nun's Priest's Tale" (pg 235).
[74] Colossians 3:16.

Someone may protest: "But what about the time God did speak to me powerfully from a randomly chosen text?"

I have no quarrel with that. The Lord is sovereign, and he may choose to speak exotically even to his most mature children. Who can deny him freedom to startle and entrance us by some curious communication? Thank God for happy surprises! May the Lord, who has often delighted me with elegant interventions, do so another thousand times!

So I have no wish to hinder him from showing his will through a "Promise Box", or by a few words of accidentally encountered scripture, or by any means he chooses. Yet if I today knew nothing more of God than those occasions has taught me, I would be ignorant indeed! My real joy in the Lord, my deepest experience of his grace, my clearest vision of his ineffable glory, has come out of prolonged meditation in the whole Bible.[75]

GUIDED BY THE WORD

The poverty of most Christians is not that they lack individual "words" from God, but that they are starved of the "Word"! Those who are weak in scripture will be inept in everything. Peter makes that plain. He describes a normal, vibrant Christian life -calling it a life of grace and peace, of divine power, splendor, excellence, godliness, and freedom. Then he reveals the source of this dynamic living: the Bible. Said Peter

> *"The more you learn about God, and about Jesus our Lord, the more grace and peace will be multiplied to you. Because of your*

---

[75] Psalm 1:1-6

> *<u>knowledge</u> of him, his divine power is able to give you everything you need for a godly life. He calls us to share his own glory and excellence, and for that reason*
>
> *he has given us <u>his priceless and incredibly great promises</u> – for <u>by these alone</u> you will be able to fend off the corrupt influence exerted against you by the passions of the world."*[76]

Four times in three verses the apostle stresses the importance of scripture to a strong Christian life. There is no way other than saturating your mind and spirit with the word of God to maintain spiritual vitality. Therefore, just as the Bible is the key to *"excellent"* (not mediocre) life in Christ, so it must be the mainstay of divine guidance. Whatever seems to come to us from God, whatever other people tell us, must be judged in the light of scripture. Anything in disagreement with God's written Word must be rejected. We sing the same refrain as the psalmist -

> *"Your word is the lamp of my feet and the light of my path!"*[77]

However - forgive me for saying it again - there is a right and a wrong way to draw wisdom out of the Bible. The worst possible method is random plucking of a text from the sacred page. Superstition, not faith, supposes that the first verse to strike your eye must be a message from God. Such practices have their roots in the lore of the ancient Romans, who sought heavenly guidance by turning haphazardly to the poetry of Virgil. That kind of

---

[76] 2 Peter 1:2-5
[77] Psalm 119:105.

awestruck gullibility has no place in Christian life. The Bible is not a Ouija board; don't poke into it blindly as though it were a lucky barrel. The ancients practiced divination by rummaging among animal entrails; some Christians subject scripture to the same kind of mindless grubbing. Small wonder if they walk in as much darkness as any heathen.

Need I remind you of that fabled fool, who in growing desperation kept stabbing his finger into his Bible? He came up with the following sequence: "Judas went and hanged himself ... Go thou and do likewise ... What thou doest, do quickly ... O wicked man, thou shalt surely die!"

Surely it is unbecoming for a mature Christian to seek guidance by legerdemain; surely it is a parody of faith to use scripture in such a pagan way. You should not approach you Bible looking for a magical word from God to spring out of a casual verse. It is usually dangerous to pluck a passage out of its context and to make it speak to a foreign set of circumstances. Guidance should flow out of a broad and deep understanding of the total message of scripture. Give yourself to constant and pervasive study of every part of scripture. That is the pathway to wisdom. Anything less is hazardous to your soul.

A BLOOD-STAINED LESSON

The ancient Jews understood the principle of discovering truth in scripture, and contrasted it with the occult superstitions of the heathen -

> *"They unrolled the scroll of the law, expecting to find the guidance that the Gentiles sought*

from their images and idols" [78]

The year was approximately 170 B.C., and the Jews were in revolt against their Seleucid oppressors. Since they were heavily outnumbered, and had few weapons, they needed guidance on how to conduct the war shrewdly and successfully. There were no living prophets in Israel to consult, so they turned to the scriptures. They searched the sacred scroll, expecting to uncover God's righteous strategy. Would it please God for them to join battle with their enemies; how should they fight; what battle plan would bring them victory?

This perception of scripture as the best place to gain wisdom had not come to them easily. It was born in the spilled blood of pious folly. The Syrians had chosen to launch their first attack on a Sabbath day. Many devout Jews, preferring death above violation of the Sabbath, refused either to fight the enemy or to defend themselves. Some of them were hoping also that God would observe their piety, and save them by a miracle. Their hope was vain, for the Syrians, finding them helpless, gleefully slaughtered men, women, and children alike.

One of the Jewish leaders, Mattathias, realized that he and his people faced utter destruction if they continued the naive policy of not fighting on the Sabbath. It was insane for them to put down their weapons and hope for supernatural rescue. So he gathered an army around him, and resolved to take the battle to the gates of the enemy, heedless of time, season, or place.[79] These were the men who turned to scripture for guidance in their conduct of the war.

---

[78] 1 Maccabees 3:48.
[79] 1 Maccabees 2:32-48.

Opening the Bible, though, was hardly enough. The naive people whom the Syrians had massacred had also quoted scripture. Therefore these new leaders determined to use the word of God more responsibly. They threw off the shackles of rigid piety; they stopped looking credulously for a miracle that would by itself make their enemies vanish.

Did they then surrender to unbelief? No, for they still trusted God to give them victory; they still expected a miracle - but one of a different kind. They understood now that they would have to fight - skillfully, astutely, and hard. What they needed was instruction in principles of justice and godliness, in precepts of faith, which would keep them allied with the Lord God. Without his help they could not win; but if they fought within a framework established by scripture, they could not lose! They knew God would support his word, when that word was rightly understood and wisely trusted; but they had also discovered, through the sanguinary slaughter of their neighbors, that the Lord has no duty to defend folly.

Wisdom waits there, for you and me to learn.

CRAVING SUCCESS

The main motivation of *"fleece"* users is a hunger for guaranteed success. Like Gideon, they refuse to act unless God shows them by a *"fleece"* that all will be well. But some things can be learned only by failure. If perfect guidance were readily and supernaturally available to every Christian, then failure would be impossible, and we would never learn some of life's deepest lessons. Solomon's comment on the human condition therefore remains true;

> *"I have also observed this happening under the sun: a swift man loses the race, and a mighty man falls in battle. I have seen hunger gripping a wise man, a brilliant man deprived of wealth, and those who are skilful stripped of honor. Time and chance happen to everyone, nor does anyone know when his hour will come."*[80]

"Time and chance happen to everyone" - so much depends upon being in the right place, or knowing the right person, at the right time! Just the other day, while watching a classical music program on television, I heard these words: "You can't predict the course of your career, no matter how talented you are. So much depends on luck!" *The speaker was Maestro Michael Tilson, guest conductor of the New World Symphony of Miami. He was addressing a group of highly skilled young musicians, who were all dreaming of gaining renown in the world of music. The maestro knew that neither talent alone, nor hard work, would bring those young people to the realization of their dreams. Some of the less skilled would gain top positions in their profession; others more talented would fail. Beyond toil or skill, their future depended upon a conjunction of things over which they had little control. Life is erratic!* "Time and chance" *play games with us all. As Charles Dickens once said,*

> *"I have been very fortunate in worldly matters; many have worked much harder and not succeeded half so well!"*[81]

---

[80] Ecclesiastes 9:11-12.
[81] Op. cit. Nonetheless, Dickens did work hard, and elsewhere in his autobiography stressed the need for diligent toil as necessary to success: "My meaning simply is, that whatever I have tried to do in life, I have tried with all my heart to do well; that whatever

The famous Clark Gable, once called "The King of Hollywood", had a similar wry estimation of his worth:

> *"The 'King' stuff is pure bull. I eat and drink and go to the bathroom just like anybody else. I'm just a lucky slob from Ohio who happened to be in the right place at the right time!"* [82]

What does it mean? Just this: we must learn to rejoice in the Lord whether or not we 'succeed". Life has crushed better men and women than you and I; people worse than we are have ridden a high wave of worldly renown! Therefore, find a nobler and better measure of yourself. Resist this world's relentless pressure to identify yourself by what you *do* and *have* rather than by what you *are*.

Werner Weinberg, a survivor of the Jewish Holocaust, wrote about the impossibility of assigning a reason, amid the complexities of life, for the fame of some and the obscurity of others. He said, *"accident and coincidence are determining forces in life."*

You may not want to be as secular as that; but in general it is true. God does not often dig an extraordinary channel for earth's rivers; he usually allows the waters to follow

---

I have devoted myself to, I have devoted myself to completely; that in great aims and in small, I have always been thoroughly in earnest. I have never believed it possible that any natural or improved ability can claim immunity from the companionship of the steady, plain, hard-working qualities, and hope to gain its end. There is no such thing as such fulfillment on this earth. Some happy talent, and some fortunate opportunity, may form the two sides of the ladder on which some men mount, but the rounds of that ladder must be made of stuff to stand wear and tear; and there is no substitute for thoroughgoing, ardent, and sincere earnestness. Never to put one hand to anything on which I could throw my whole self; and never to affect depreciation of my work, whatever it was; I find, now, to have been one of my golden rules." (Ibid., pg. 147,148). Dickens' rule, "never to affect depreciation of my work," merits pondering.

[82] I have lost the source of this quote.

their natural course. Thus the events of life hew their own channel; sometimes through verdant fields, sometimes through fetid swamps. We are carried along by the stream, and often find that injustice and unfairness abound. Christians discover that they are not immune from their neighbors' pain -

> *"None of us can live, nor even die, wholly in charge of our own destiny. Whether we like it or not, our lives are linked with those around us."* [83]

But always remember: finally there can be no failure for any person who is united with Christ by faith. For us, death is an open doorway to resurrection; for us, there is no defeat but only victory!

Here is the challenge for faith: to believe that Christ transforms every happening, every circumstance, into an upward step on the stairway to Paradise!

FORCING THE ISSUE

Fleece-users often have another motive: to compel God to give an answer within a certain time, as though the Almighty can be held to some human agenda. Long ago, the Jews saw the folly of that idea. They told the story of how Judith rebuked the elders of her city because they had set a five-day time limit on God -

> *"Listen to me, magistrates of Bethulia. Who gave you the right...to make this sworn promise to surrender our town to the enemy if God fails to help us within so many days?*

---

[83] Romans 14:7.

You even made God a partner in your oath! How dare you test God like this! Would you make yourself greater than he is? Do you think you are better than anyone else? Do you think you can put the Almighty on trial?

How ignorant you are! Look, you can't even fathom the human heart, nor read even another man's thoughts – how then do you expect to understand the mind of God? If the creature baffles your wisdom, how will you ever probe the Creator? I warn you my friends, stop provoking the anger of the Lord our God. Suppose he does not choose to help us within your limit of five days? Does he not have the right to rescue us whenever he pleases; or, if he chooses, to let our enemies destroy us? Will you argue with God" Will you tell him what he can do? <u>He is not someone like you, who can be intimidated with threats. You can't drive a bargain with him, as though he were a merchant. Stop trying to impose conditions on the Lord God!</u> We can do nothing except call upon him to help us and then wait for his deliverance. He will hear our cry, and if it please him, he will rescue us"[84]

Need I say more? Think about the wisdom of the old rabbis. It is no less valid now than it was then.

---

[84] Judith 7:30-32; 8:11-16. Note, though, that Judith herself didn't sit around wringing her hands, praying desperately, and waiting for a miracle. She implemented a shrewd and daring plan that enabled her to murder the enemy general and rout his army. The story, of course, is fictitious, but its moral and spiritual lessons remain important.

Alison's Story

SORROW TURNED TO JOY!
(1955-1970)

Something was seriously wrong! Ken and I had always wanted a large family. During our courtship we had joked about having twelve children after our marriage, and had both eagerly looked forward to lots of babies.

We had one dear little son, but he was growing older and we wanted to give him a brother or sister to enjoy.

Tragedy struck! I became pregnant only to lose the baby at two months. Later I became pregnant again only to lose yet another child.

Looking back now over the years I can recognize the deep work done in us by these happenings. But then I could not see the coming heartbreak or the overwhelming joy of God's final triumph over all our despair. I know why God will not let us look too far ahead: we could not bear the knowledge!

I can also see how the Father uses tragedy to build character, compassion, and toughness of spirit into his people. His goal is to refine and mould them into strong men and women of God.

He does not personally send illness or accident. These are just part of life. But he does use them. Nothing is wasted. The Lord weaves every thread of experience into the fabric of our personality as we learn to yield ourselves to him and to rely on him totally.

My doctor discovered I had some small fibroid tumors and he wanted to operate, but I refused. I preferred to believe God for my healing and began to fast and pray.

God has healed my body and met our physical needs often, each in a new and different way.

I felt wonderful after my fast, and had boundless energy. Scriptures filled my mind; I allowed no negative thoughts to enter. Life was good. Nine months later I learned that God had answered prayer, and that the tumors had disappeared. But by then it didn't seem to matter very much. A new sorrow had fallen upon us, casting a bleak shadow over our happiness. Our home would never be the same again.

GAVIN IS BORN, AND DIES (1957-1961)

We had left our first church in Ballarat and moved to a young church in Springvale, a hundred miles away. There, on the second of November, I gave birth by caesarian section to a dear little four-and-a-half pound baby boy. He was with us just two days.

On the fourth of November he went to be with Jesus. Heaven will always seem very near to us because one of our little one is there waiting for us. We named him Gavin James and laid him to rest in a tiny suburban Anglican Church cemetery.

Little Gavin's life was so brief because of a condition called Placentia Preavia. I had lost part of the placenta at six months and then he had been born by caesarian section at seven and a half months. He was terribly

Discovery

bruised, and died two days later.

We were devastated. As I lay there in hospital, all I could say was "Why, Lord, why did you allow this to happen to us?"

Ken tried to comfort me.

"I don't know why, but I do know this," he said, "one day God will explain everything."

Clinging to this thought brought comfort to me over the next painful weeks and months.

"God, my little one will never know the joys of this life. He will never be able to play ball, or eat chocolate, or gambol in the waves of the sea. He will never laugh and play with his older brother."

"Neither will he have to experience any sorrow," was the gentle reply.

Each time I closed my eyes I was given a picture of Jesus holding my little baby close in his arms. He seemed to say that baby Gavin was safe with him; and with that I must be content.

One day, lying on my hospital bed, I watched two little sparrows flirting, their tails bobbing, and twittering happily as they gathered material for their nest.

"Life goes on," I thought. "How good God is to give me this message through two of his smallest and humblest creatures."

SHARON IS BORN

If Ken and I could have seen into the future during those dark days, we would have been consoled. God would recompense us for the suffering we were going through. He was to grant us not only a darling daughter, but two more precious sons to give us much happiness.

Before then, however, we had to work through a great test of our faith and to gain an enormous victory for the Lord. It would be a vindication of God's healing power, which he would allow us to take around the world. Through this testimony many other couples, yearning for children, would find faith to have their prayers answered by God.

You will find that story in a later Interlude; but meanwhile, I needed a period of healing and recuperation. The doctor assured me I had no tumors. The reason for my miscarriages was still a mystery to him.

During the following year I built up my strength. We also moved to Adelaide, where Ken was asked to become an assistant pastor in our home church, under Pastor Leo Harris.[85]

Finally, when Dale was five and a half years of age, we were able to place in his arms a little sister. Sharon Elizabeth Rae. As I write, she is serving God, with her husband Pastor David Jones, in San Diego, USA. To bear her I had to remain bedfast for seven months (from when I was six weeks pregnant until she was born at eight and a half months). Many times it seemed we would lose her, but always God intervened, and at last she was born

---

[85] Founder of the Christian Revival Crusade in Australia, and the founder and pastor of the great Adelaide Crusade Centre.

safely.

The mystery of my miscarriages was also revealed. I had RH-negative blood and had built up antibodies against my babies. Sharon had to have her blood exchanged when she was two days of age. After that all was well. We were happy and contented. Our little family was growing.

Dr. Ken Chant

Fourth Fallacy

OPEN DOORS REVEAL THE WILL OF GOD"

Once upon a time there was a pious young man who endlessly asked God for instructions: shall I do this? do you want me to go here? can I buy this? do you want me to give that? - and on, and on. One day he was on his knees as usual, bombarding heaven with many petitions, when he heard an exasperated voice: *"Enough already, son! Decide for yourself what you want to do. I'm your Father, not your mother!"*[86]

It was time for the lad to make some decisions of his own! Only the irresponsible, or the fearful, wait indefinitely for some kind of supernatural command. Genuine faith prefers to step out and go on, believing that God (even if unseen, unfelt, unheard) has ultimate control over each new day. Therefore all will be well. In pitch darkness we sing our hope of his redeeming love.[87]

Against that teaching stand those whose criteria for discerning the will of God are open or closed "doors". Is that wrong? Not always, for sometimes the shape of circumstances *may* show the divine purpose; a "closed door", an "open door", *may* point you in the direction God wants you to go. Indeed, the same could be said of all the

---

[86] An obviously mythical story, told to me by my nephew Michael. I suppose he in turn heard it from someone else.
[87] Job 35:10; Psalm 42:8

"fallacies" we are looking at in this book. None of them are wholly wrong. Many times they are God's chosen method to reveal his will. The fallacy lies not so much in the rules themselves as in giving them an *absolute* value, as though they were always true and could always be relied upon. Any one of them (or all of them together) may at times be a useful indicator of the purpose of God; but if you lean too heavily upon them they will pierce your hand.

So "an open door" may here or there show you which way the Lord wants you to go. But there will be other times when you will have to act against all comfort, and risk everything, to do God's best. Sometimes you must press ahead, though every *"door"* seems closed. If it won't open, kick it down!

Better still, try looking, not for a "door", but for a "need" that you are able, with your particular gifts, to meet. Here is a practical formula: *need + ability = opportunity!* If that prescription fits your present situation, then set to work! No further approval from heaven is necessary. If perchance the Lord *does* have another task for you to do, he will accept the responsibility of directing you to it.

Suppose several opportunities stand in front of you? Then choose the one that is most congenial. Only a masochist deliberately seeks discomfort, hardship, or pain, without any good reason for it. If you can serve God pleasantly and prosperously, then do so. How foolish, if not paranoid, to crave suffering! Ask the Lord rather for peace and plenty. He will not withhold his bounteous gifts except for an adequate purpose. But be warned: if you *really* set yourself to serve the King, his many foes will soon be yapping at your heels! You may then have to look higher than this earth for lasting consolation and happiness![88]

A LION IN THE STREET!

Here is a corrective text for people who insist upon standing still until God opens a "door" for them -

> "If you sit around waiting for perfect conditions to arrive, you will never get anything done."*[89]*

Don't join those pious souls who are always looking for an auspicious sign, some favorable augur from heaven, a message in the clouds, a wide open door, before they dare to act. Banish any readiness to invent barriers where there are none. Excuses are never lacking for those who cannot or will not either trust the Lord or obey him.

Then there are those who see perils in every shadow; even broad daylight frightens them. Solomon mocked the exaggerated fears of such people. They are as ridiculous (he said) as an idler who refuses to go to work because a lion might be waiting to devour him![90]

Then there are others, eager to hear from God, who see an omen in every strange happening. The littlest departure from normal is enough to persuade them the Lord has spoken, telling them to go forward, or back, or to turn this way or that. How foolish to see the beckoning finger of God where it does not exist!

Charles Kingsley, in his account of the Elizabethan mariner, John Oxenham, poked a mocking finger at

---

[88] John 16:33.
[89] Ecclesiastes 11:4; from Kenneth Taylor's paraphrase.
[90] Proverbs 22:13; 26:13.

people who allow themselves to be controlled by some kind of "omen". The worthy captain had seen a spectral white bird and was terrified by the vision, for its appearance was traditionally thought to presage a death in his family. Sir Richard Grenville, hearing about this, scorned the seaman's fears –

> *"But, indeed, I make no account of omens. When God is ready for each man, then he must go; and when can he go better?"*
>
> *"But,"* said Mr. Leigh, who entered, *"I have seen, and especially when I was in Italy, omens and prophecies before now beget their own fulfillment, by driving men into recklessness, and making them run headlong upon that very ruin which, as they fancied, was running upon them."*
>
> *"And which,"* said Sir Richard, *"they might have avoided if, instead of trusting in I know not what dumb and stark destiny, they had trusted in the living God, by faith in whom men may remove mountains, and quench fire, and put to flight the armies of the alien!"*[91]

How true it is that omens tend to have a self-fulfilling effect. Those who are governed by them give life to them, which otherwise they would not have. The Book of Proverbs *again comes to our rescue. Have you ever noticed the sensible temper of that book? It is not anti-supernatural, yet neither does it favor a naively miraculous approach to life. Solomon knew nothing about surrendering responsibility for personal decision-making to signs and wonders. He had scant patience with the*

---

[91] Westward Ho!, Chapter One.

supernaturalism that, disdaining ordinary methods, looks only for miracles to meet human need.

Wherever you turn in Proverbs, you find common-sense advice on how to manage your affairs shrewdly, carefully, and profitably. The various writers honor God, they trust his Providence, they anticipate his blessing; yet they seldom expect him to influence the course of events by some direct action. They do not plan their daily lives within a framework of supernatural intervention. The hand of God, according to Proverbs, mostly works behind the scenes, unseen and unfelt, for the Lord more often uses earthly than heavenly means to fulfill his will.

Perhaps someone scorns Proverbs because of its Old Testament setting? Well then, look at Paul -

STOPPED BY SATAN

"We urgently wanted to come to you, but Satan stopped us."[92]

If you have ever read any science fiction, or watched *Star Trek* on television, you have met the idea of a "force field" - an invisible and impenetrable high-energy barrier, produced by some futuristic device. Paul uses a word in the above text that is a kind of first-century equivalent to the idea of a "force-field". In Bible days it described a military road-block, designed to stop an invading army. But the modern idea of an invisible barrier better captures the sense Paul had in mind, that is, *"a spiritual blockade imposed by the devil."*

"Satan has stopped us!" he exclaimed. "Whenever we try

---

[92] 1 Thessalonians 2:18.

to go forward we run into this hellish wall, and we can't find any way to break through it. Despite our constant prayers, day and night, the devil's blockade stands immovable. Satan has stopped us dead in our tracks!"

Plainly the great apostle was not familiar with the latest book on "the power of a positive confession!" We can hardly believe he made such a negative statement! Pardon us for intruding, Paul, but we urge you to get to the nearest "faith-convention". Hasn't anyone told you how to speak nothing but the word of God? Don't you know you are glorifying the devil when you confess what he has done? Don't you realize, every time you admit that Satan has bush-whacked you, you give him more power? You are talking yourself into defeat! Get hold of your mouth, Paul! That kind of negative confession will bring you nothing but trouble!

Of course, those words are not mine; but there *are* people who do think like that, and they are much bothered by Paul's stark confession. If you can't say something positive, they argue, then don't say anything. Better to keep your lips closed than to speak openly about fear or failure. And especially, they say, *never* admit that the devil has got the upper hand on you!

Paul would agree with them - in part; for aside from Jesus, no other man has ever known more than he about the authority of God's word, or more successfully spoken miracles into existence by that word. In the following paragraphs I will show you just how effectively Paul did use powerful affirmations to turn defeat into victory. But he also avoided the folly of allowing his commitment to a "positive confession" to blind his sense of reality.

Honesty is never a bad policy. Paul never imagined that

the truth would anger God; therefore he could always state facts without apology.

How hard that would be in some places!

There are churches where a pastor would lose his job if he echoed Paul, *"Satan stopped me!"* - especially if he failed to clutter his admission with a parade of excuses. Among such congregations, to get sick is a heresy, to fail is a sin, to be afraid is blasphemy, to make a "negative" statement is obscenity.

Such spiritual taboos would have been repulsive to Paul. *"Satan stopped me,"* pronounced the great apostle, offering no explanation. *"Satan stopped me,"* he calmly declared, with no blush of shame. *"Satan stopped me,"* was his honest statement, never supposing such frankness could harm him.

Has Satan "stopped" *you*?

Perhaps there is a wall of darkness around you, a barrier of fear, a demonic blockade stifling your prayers. The real issue is not whether you admit that the devil is crushing you, but what is your faith-response to the satanic siege? The passage of scripture from which our text comes suggests four doors of faith you can walk through, four wall-breaching "confessions" you can always make:

Satan May Stop Me - He Cannot Discourage Me

> *"Because we are bereft of you, dear friends, we feel like parents whose children have been torn away from them. Our hearts are still with you, though we have been physically parted from each other for a short time. Yes, a passionate longing to be with you burns inside*

> us! We have explored every possibility and almost exhausted our strength trying to come to you - you will never know how hard we have tried! I myself, even I, Paul, have tried again and again to come to you. But Satan stopped us."[93]

What fervent, unrestrained language! Paul uses the common word for "lust"[94] to describe his yearning to get back to Thessalonica. No other term was strong enough for him. Again, in the middle of the paragraph, he breaks passionately away from the formal "we" to an informal "I, even I, Paul." How earnestly he presses his desire! Yet despite their ardent wishes, despite exerting all their skill, despite zealously and repeatedly trying to surmount the barrier, Paul and his companions were thwarted at every turn by Satan!

Is anyone immune from that frustration? The devil plants his thorny hedges around all of us from time to time. Why bother to deny it? Satan has ways of reaching out to harm us financially, to wreck our well-laid plans, to impose sickness, to stymie our best efforts to serve God. But don't be discouraged! Take heart (like Paul) and press on. There are ways to get around the devil's roadblocks. He might think he has built an immovable obstacle, but we have on our side an irresistible force! If something "irresistible" exists, then nothing is "immovable"! In the end, the worst of Satan's impediments must yield before Jesus' name!

How well Paul displayed that kind of unwavering

---

[93] Ibid. verses 17,18.
[94] The word translated as "passionate longing" above occurs 37 times in the New Testament, 34 of them having the meaning "lust"; for example, as in 1 Thessalonians 4:5.

confidence a few sentences later in his letter -

> *"How can we ever thank God enough for you! Because of you, we feel abounding happiness in the presence of God. That is why, night and day we are begging God to let us come to you in person, so that we may mend any breaches that remain in your faith. Oh, that our God and Father himself, and our Lord Jesus, would bring us straight to you again!"*[95]

Can you doubt that Paul expected his prayer to be answered? He knew that sooner or later the Father would give him his heart's desire. So he refused to be discouraged. He continued to make merry before the throne of God. So long as he could *pray* he had a resource available to him that mocked all the Enemy's pretensions to power!

Can *you* still pray? Then you too can cast aside depression and helplessness, and laugh at the devil. Then you will also affirm that;

Satan May Stop Me - He Cannot Deny Me

Luke tells the dramatic story in *Acts 17:1-10* of the founding of the church at Thessalonica. After only three weeks Paul had established a congregation in the home of Jason, along with miracles, tumults, and riots! The level of violence continued to rise, until the small, threatened congregation had to steal Paul out of the city by night and send him off to Berea. Later, when he wrote his first letter to the Thessalonians, he still had not been able to return to them.

---

[95] 3:9-11.

Meanwhile, enemies had spread vicious rumors against the apostle, accusing him of being a false teacher, and of cravenly getting all the money he could out of the young church before running away. So Paul was desperately anxious to get back to Thessalonica, both to nurture the new Christians and to squash those lies. He had tried "again and again", only to be prevented every time.

How did the devil stop him? We don't know. The problem may have been the bond Jason had to pay to the magistrates, complicated by a family relationship between him and Paul. Jason found himself responsible for maintaining the peace, probably by keeping his relative out of the city.[96] Perhaps Paul had pleaded frequently, but without success, for the ban against him returning to Thessalonica to be lifted.

However, whatever the "stopping force" was, Paul did eventually overcome it; for on his third missionary journey he visited Macedonia again, and preached there with powerful effect![97] What was the key to his triumph? Undoubtedly, his refusal to let go of the word God had given him earlier. The Lord had promised him that he would preach in Macedonia and build many churches there,[98] so he *"resolved in the Spirit to travel through Macedonia."*[99] Nothing could deter him. Nothing could persuade him to abandon the heavenly vision. Nothing could force him to deny the promise he had received. He set himself to affirm that promise until it had been fulfilled to his satisfaction.

---

[96] Acts 17:6,9; Romans 16:21. Jason may have been a cousin of Paul's, or perhaps related to him through marriage.
[97] Acts 19:21-22; 20:1-3.
[98] Acts 16:9-10.
[99] Acts 19:21.

Paul's unyielding trust in the word of God shines brightly in one phrase in our text passage. He lamented the pain his continued forced separation from his friends was causing him, and he angrily blamed Satan for it. Nonetheless, he declared emphatically, it would last only for *"a short time"*.[100] By faith Paul announced that every devilish barricade would eventually fall and the word of God would stand triumphant. He was certain of it! Nothing could prevent it! God's word believed and spoken is God's word fulfilled!

That is a good example for anyone to follow!

Satan May Stop Me - He Cannot Deprive Me

Jesus used one noun to express all the misery the devil has brought upon mankind: he called Satan the *"Thief"*. What sorrow is not found there? Theft is the common pain, the burning grief of every man and woman. We are robbed of our holiness and happiness, of our health and prosperity, of our love and our laughter, of our dreams and our destiny. No one escapes this depredation; and God's children, who understand more finely what life should be, feel the loss more keenly.

Robert Browning, in his beautiful reflection *The Last Ride Together*, captured this universal privation -

> Fail I alone, in words and deeds?
> Why, all men strive, and who succeeds?
>
> I thought, - All labor, yet no less
> Bear up beneath their unsuccess.
> Look at the end of work, contrast

---

[100] 1 Thessalonians 2:17.

> The petty done, the undone vast,
> This present of theirs with the hopeful past!
>
> What hand and brain went ever paired?
> What heart alike conceived and dared?
> What act proved all its thought had been?
> What will but felt the fleshly screen?

Have you not found it so? Who, starting on their pilgrim path, has not dreamed wonderful dreams of empires wrought, castles built, dragons defeated, fabulous deeds done for the glory of God? Yet at the end of the journey, how petty the done seems against the immensity of the undone; how dismal the present seems against the radiant light of yesterday's hopes!

No hand, as the poet said, has ever built all that the mind imagined; no heart has ever dared all that it has dreamed; no action has ever equaled the aspirations that drove it; no zeal has ever fully overcome the leaden weight of the flesh. Amid the sweetest fortune and favor of this life there is always a timbre of grief. Love remains debtor to its promised joy; ashes embitter the taste of ambition's fulfillment; happiness crumbles beneath the shadow of mortality; the grave digs a mocking end to every earthly pretension.

Suddenly, just as despair begins to chill the soul, faith hears another voice. It cries: *Satan can rob you only on the surface!* The Thief carries off only life's pebbles! Your real treasure lies where no bandit can touch it or moth consume, nor rust corrupt![101]

That is why Paul wrote -

---
[101] Luke 12:33.

"Since you have been lifted out of death with Christ, turn your eyes toward heaven, for Christ is there, sitting at God's right hand. Fix your minds on that higher plane, not down here on earth. Don't you realize this: you began by dying with Christ, but now your true life is hidden with Christ in God? When Christ, who is our true life, suddenly appears, then you too will appear with him, clothed in the same glory!"[102]

Do you understand those things? If you do, then you really won't care very much what happens to you during the short span of your mortal life. Your lasting happiness finds its home beyond time in eternity, and beyond earth in heaven.

With arresting drama Paul demonstrates this ineradicable source of joy. He has just said, "*Satan stopped us.*" What would you expect his next words to be? Some angry protest? A gloomy resignation to disappointment? A hasty justification of his weakness? Perhaps all those. Nor would any of them seem surprising if spoken by a lesser Christian.

But Paul, unlike Caesar, had an "ambition made of sterner stuff"![103] He was a real Christian. He had his priorities right. So what did he say? His response is startling. Tumbling right on top of his exasperated confession of satanic delay come the festive words: *"hope ... delight ... crown ... pride ... glory ... joy!"*[104] There is no pause, no hiatus, no complaint, no interval. Satan may

---
[102] Colossians 3:1-4.
[103] Shakespeare, Julius Caesar III,ii,97. Mark Anthony is speaking ironically, noting how Caesar wept when he saw the suffering of the poor.
[104] 1 Thessalonians 2:18-20.

have stopped Paul, but never for a moment had the Enemy quenched his irrepressible assurance in the Lord! The apostle remains rich beyond all telling. He has treasure beyond all counting. The superlatives pile on top of each other, his exuberance cannot be stifled, his courage is dauntless. How could it be otherwise? His mind was "fixed on that higher plane, not down here on earth"!

Nothing therefore could long repress the apostle's ebullient faith. Let the rank Burglar do his worst. In the end his most savage robberies are mere pennies taken out of a limitless fortune! Why should we regret the loss of a little petty cash when we still possess a mountain of gold? Let the devil take all he can; we will still laugh. He has not diminished by so much as a grain of dust our riches of hope in the gospel, our treasure of joy in Christ, or our wealth of delight in the kingdom. Our crown of righteousness sits firm, our pride in God unbowed, our glory in heaven for ever undimmed. Our real coffers remain always full, for ever beyond the Robber's greed!

Here is a cheerful irony: those are most likely to preserve their happiness on earth who care least about it! The best protection you can put around your worldly wealth is to turn your eye from those moldering rags to the endless riches that are yours in the heavenlies in Christ.[105] Concentrate on this life and you will lose it all – if not this side of the grace, then on the other. Concentrate on the realm above, and probably you will preserve your prosperity here while building a greater estate there. Yet even if you seem to lose your earthly property, you will have kept it; for what you surrender here in the name of the Lord will rebound to your greater treasure there!

---

[105] Proverbs 11:24; Luke 12:16-31; plus many other references.

Satan May Stop Me - He Cannot Defeat Me

Sir Thomas Malory's Le Morte D'Arthur[106] has probably influenced western culture more than any other book except the Bible. Swords clash, arrows whir, glittering knights ride out to rescue fair maidens, dragons belch fire, giants roar, the Holy Grail beckons, dreadful battles are fought - wonderful adventures spring out of every page.

Malory tells how the boy Arthur pulled the enchanted sword Excalibur out of its imprisoning stone. This feat marked him as the child destined to be king, and Arthur was at once acclaimed as the sovereign lord of all England. But he was tender in years and unskilled in war. Many great barons refused to swear allegiance to such a stripling, and a terrible civil war began. Arthur fared badly. Victory upon victory went to the rebellious lords, until the boy king found himself besieged in the last of his castles. There he sat, trembling and dismayed, until suddenly Merlin, the greatest of magicians, appeared before him. The wizard rebuked the frightened lad, and (says Malory) "bade him to fear not, but to come out boldly and speak to them and spare them not, but to answer them as their king and chieftain: `For ye shall overcome them all, whether they wish it or wish it not!'"

Arthur took courage, crossed the drawbridge, and confronted the attacking host alone. Excalibur flashed in the sunlight, dazzling, mysterious, awful, and suddenly the besieging host fell before the young king like grass bending beneath a violent wind. The legend of Camelot was born.

---

[106] Op. cit.

When I first read Merlin's rebuke of the frightened boy, I was deeply stirred. I thought about myself and other Christians, often cowed by the enemy, yielding to his threats, surrendering to his bribery, meekly accepting his chains. The devil rattles his weapons of sickness and sin, of fear and poverty, and God's brave warriors at once discard their shields, cast off their armor, throw away their weapons, and fling themselves at the enemy's feet!

But we have a magic sword, our own true Excalibur, a blade infinitely mightier than Arthur's mythical weapon.[107] It is the Word of God, against whose sharp edge Satan has no defense! Let us then stand firm, and speak bravely. Are we not kings and priests before our God?[108] Have we not a divine right to domineer every dark power? Then sally forth and challenge the Foe! Demand that he fall back! Seize from him all that he has stolen! Force every dark spirit to give way in Jesus' name. Our Sovereign Lord says: "*You will overcome them all, whether they wish it or wish it not!*"[109]

That is what Paul did. He continued to answer his terrible foe as his "king and chieftain". Satan had to yield. The barrier was torn aside. The apostle of God went back to Thessalonica. His prayers were fully answered.

OPEN YOUR OWN DOOR

But having said all that, this fact remains: when he wrote to the Thessalonians Paul was still trapped behind that satanic barrier, unable to fulfill his God-given ministry.

---

[107] Ephesians 6:17.
[108] 1 Peter 2:9.
[109] Luke 10:18-19.

The delay may only have been temporary, but it was nonetheless baffling and painful. Paul found the door closed fast, and his way completely blocked. Even God seemed against him, for although the apostle and his companions had been "Praying fervently night and day" for a way to open for them to preach in Thessalonica[110] heaven remained silent. The devil still seemed firmly in control.

Paul was in a torment of frustration. He felt that he could *"bear it no longer."*[111] What should he do? Resign himself to the inevitable and wait patiently for God to answer his prayers? Call more prayer-partners together to storm the heavenlies until they broke down the walls? Pull back for a time, quiet his spirit, and allow the Holy Spirit to whisper a word of guidance? Get furious with the devil, and stir up a hurricane of rebuke against every opposing demon?

Paul could have done all those things. He did none of them. Instead, he pondered the matter, until he hit upon a shrewd plan to outwit both Satan and the Roman authorities.

> *"Since I could no longer bear the pain of our separation. I decided to remain alone in Athens and to send Timothy in my place. He is a true brother, who serves God in the gospel of Christ, so I trusted him to strengthen your faith and to urge you not to let these*

---

[110] 1 Thessalonians 3:10. Note how this verse makes nonsense of the idea that to pray more than once for something is to pray in unbelief. When he wanted something with enough passion, Paul did not hesitate to barrage heaven with prayers "day and night"! Jesus taught the same, Luke 11:9-12; 18:1-7.

[111] Verses 1,5.

> *hardships unsettle you. You already know that suffering is inescapable, for we warned you about this when we were still with you. Now it has happened, just as we said. That is why, driven by a burning need to know how you were faring, I sent Timothy to you. I was anxious lest the Tempter had enticed you away, thus undoing all our work among you"*[112]

So there is Paul, stopped by the devil, worried about his friends, constantly hounded by persecutors, and praying day and night (so far without success) for God to open the way for him to visit Thessalonica himself. What does he do? He finally takes matters into his own hands. Since *he* couldn't go, let another go instead! So he sent Timothy, while he (Paul) waited in Athens alone. This was not something God told him to do. It just seemed like a good idea, which was certainly better than doing nothing!

Can you find any hint in that passage of the apostle seeking some special word or direction from heaven, or refusing to act until the way before him was smooth?

Certainly he prayed, constantly, fervently, as every Christian should. He prayed with unshakable confidence, knowing that God would eventually give him his heart's desire. He prayed because he knew he could never get to Thessalonica unless the Lord were willing. He prayed because prayer was the only way to test the divine willingness, and to gain heaven's help. So he prayed, and

---

[112] Verses 1-5. The apostle's tactic, by the way, was successful. Timothy spent some time in Thessalonica, without arousing any opposition, and brought back to Paul a glowing report (verses 6-9).

told his friends he was praying -

> *"Night and day we are begging God to let us come to you in person, so that we may mend any breaches that remain in your faith. Oh, that our God and Father himself, and our Lord Jesus, would bring us straight to you again!"*[113]

Paul knew that his prayer would sooner or later be granted; nonetheless, he did not think prayer would rid him of all trouble,[114] nor was it a substitute for taking some useful action himself. Paul was quite willing to act before an answer had come from heaven. He felt no obligation to wait until he had received some "word" of divine guidance, or until some "door" supernaturally opened for him. While there has never been a more truly spiritual man, Paul was also a thoroughly pragmatic activist. He did for himself whatever he could do; only what he could not do was he content to leave wholly in God's hands. True, he was always ready for a miracle, always listening for a confided word from the Spirit; but meanwhile he got on with the job, using every resource or skill at his disposal.

Is there any reason why you shouldn't do the same?

---

[113] Verses 10-11.
[114] "Suffering and affliction," said Paul, "are ordained for us Christians; they are our lot in life" (verses 3,4,7).

Alison's Story

THE HOLY SPIRIT TO THE RESCUE! (Adelaide 1957-1962)

A lady called the church office, requesting a pastoral visit. At first Ken said that he would go, but after hanging up the phone he felt a check in his spirit. So he asked another pastor, who was already planning to take his wife out for the evening, to go in his place. The two of them agreed to visit the lady briefly on the way to their dinner engagement.

When the couple arrived at the woman's house they walked together to the door and rang the bell. She was, of course, expecting Ken. As soon as the bell rang, she flung open the door and stood there - stark naked! Quickly the pastor's wife pushed her inside, slammed the front door on her husband, hurried the lady into a bedroom, wrapped her in a blanket, and proceeded to give her a lecture she would never forget!

How thankful Ken was when he heard what had happened. God had given him extraordinary guidance, prompting him in his spirit not to visit his parishioner that night. What if Ken had not listened? Even had he resisted the wiles of the naked lady, she had only to call out and his ministry would have been ruined. Who would have believed him? It would have been his word against hers. He was only twenty-seven, and she was a beautiful young woman.

Some time later we realized how driven she had been by Satan, for she had a complete mental breakdown, and had to be hospitalized. But the Father showed her mercy. She regained her health, both mentally and spiritually, and eventually came back to the church.

AN AMAZING MIRACLE!

"Barry, I really don't think you should ride your motor-bike today," I cautioned. "You have had a fever for three days and have taken nothing but liquids. Surely it would be wiser to stay home this Sunday?"

But Ken's younger brother Barry was both devout and zealous. Insisting he would be fine, he climbed on his bike and roared off to church.

We had moved to Adelaide from Ballarat, and this was our first year working under Pastor Leo Harris. Barry was living with us, while he attended university.

After Barry had ridden away, we left for church in our car, arrived there, and the service began. Suddenly, two policemen appeared at the door. They had come to report a terrible accident. Barry had blacked out as he was traveling down the road, his motor bike had run into a telephone pole, and he was in hospital with multiple injuries. The doctors did not expect him to live through the night.

Ken and I were rushed to the hospital to sign the necessary permission forms, and the surgeons began the task of putting Barry back together. His spleen was pulverized and had to be removed; he had broken vertebrae, a broken arm, his kidneys were damaged, along with other injuries, and of course he was still weak from the fever he had had for the past few days.

Against expectation, and - we believe - in answer to prayer, he survived through the night. The surgeon said, if Barry had not been a clean-living young man he could not have done it.

I don't have space here to tell the full story, and will have to be content with saying that God gave Barry an astonishing miracle. One result of the accident was to kill the nerves in his upper arm, which shriveled the muscles, and made his arm useless. The specialist said he would never be able to move it again from the shoulder. Within three months Barry was back at university, his arm revitalized and functioning fully, his other injuries healed, his health and strength restored! There was no other explanation: God had marvelously answered prayer!

While Barry was in hospital the Lord gave me a dream. It was so vivid; I can still remember it perfectly after 30 years. I saw Barry married to his fiancée, Vanessa, and she was serving dinner to her family. Three children were seated at the table with them. I took particular note that there were three children, and that two were aged about 12, while the third was much younger, still in a high chair.

I interpreted this dream as a comforting message from the Lord for Vanessa that Barry would recover. She had been suffering great agonies of spirit as Barry was struggling for his life in hospital. My dream showed that he and Vanessa would marry, and they would have three children. Fifteen years later the Lord brought this dream to my remembrance, and I realized how accurate it had been. They do have three children, two of whom were born early in their marriage, and the third some ten years later. Now of course the older children have married and have children of their own.

EXTRAORDINARY GUIDANCE!

My pregnancy with Sharon occurred during a difficult time in Ken's ministry. Pastor Leo Harris, our senior pastor, had many invitations to preach all over the USA. He decided to accept them, and with his wife Belle, and their daughter Cherith, set the date for their departure.

We disclosed the news of my pregnancy, which was already proving to be a difficult one, but after some discussion we all decided that Leo and Belle should go ahead with their plans. We agreed to trust the Lord for my baby to be born normally. Knowing that they were praying earnestly for us, and that everywhere they ministered in the USA others would also seek the Lord on our behalf, was a great comfort to me as the trying months progressed.

The church, about 500 strong, was left in Ken's hands. He was 27 years old. Added to the church was a Bible college, a widely circulated magazine, and a nation-wide radio network. Even with a strong team of dedicated men to help him, it was a daunting task.

Half-way through the year, when the Harris's had been gone about 6 months, Ken began to undergo a severe trial. He felt he could not burden me with it because of my pregnancy, so he battled it alone.

The test was this: his faith gave way, and he no longer

believed in anything! Nothing had any meaning for him. He could not feel a particle of assurance! He reached out for God, and could not touch him! The sky was like brass above him and the earth as iron beneath his feet. Yet he continued preaching, praying for the people, teaching in the Bible college, publishing the magazine, speaking on radio, and running the church.

He knew instinctively that if he continued to do the work he'd been called to do that eventually he would come through and regain his faith. So despite the dark shadow that was on his spirit, he persevered in prayer and ministry.

For three months he suffered, until finally God lifted the veil and he could see again with the eye of faith. Now followed a series of miracles that were many and diverse in nature: blind and deaf people were cured through prayer; some people with cancer were made whole; other illnesses were overcome; and we had the ongoing miracle of the baby in my womb being preserved month after month, despite the complication of my RH-negative blood!

Ken had not prayed for this breakthrough; it came unsought because he stuck steadfastly to the principle of believing that he was in the centre of God's will. The Father then had to get him there and keep him there!

When the Harris's returned we were able to share with them the great things the Lord had done. We were glad to hand back to them a church that had grown in numbers, and we rejoiced together in our God, who is always there, and who does all things well.

Fifth Fallacy

GOD HAS A BLUEPRINT FOR MY MINISTRY!"

Some years ago I joined the ministry team of a church that had a thousand members. Imagine my astonishment when I found no less than eight unplaced preachers sitting in the pews, worshipping with the people each Sunday. Those pastors all wanted to get back into active ministry, but they were waiting for some "word" from heaven, or for a "call" from a "good" church. Their attitude disturbed me. Having once been "called" by the Holy Spirit to preach the gospel, why should they need any further assignment? Just get out and do it! If an existing church won't call you, then build your own! If no one offers you a pulpit, find a street corner! In a city of two million souls, how could there be any lack of opportunity to be about the King's business?

Yet there are many (like those eight ministers) who will not venture into any new activity without a specific mandate from God. They might agree that God's purpose for our *personal lives* is flexible, but they deny any freedom to choose one's *Christian service*. Is that true? How much does the Lord want to control your work in the church? How do you discover your proper place in the kingdom? How do you learn what God has called you to do?

BEGIN ON EARTH

Your perception of the will of God should begin on earth, not in heaven; with yourself, what you already are, not with some extraordinary miracle or strange omen. Whatever later fiat may reach you from heaven will normally build upon, not countermand, what you have now. God's purpose for your life probably will start with the things he gave you in the womb, with your existing talents and temperament. He is more likely to begin with the natural and then add the supernatural, than the reverse.

Sometimes, unhappily, we refuse to see what is plainly before our faces. So then, when he cannot get our attention any other way, the Lord may have to assault us supernaturally. But that is hardly a mark of spiritual maturity. Rather, it shows stubbornness and willful deafness! Look at Balaam's donkey. What better example is there of God imposing an unfamiliar task upon an unlikely servant?[115] Even today the Lord cannot sometimes avoid calling a donkey to do a prophet's work! But he usually prefers a skilled man or woman to an unskilled ass!

Does that mean God never wants to go against nature, that he is always reluctant to give someone an exotic task? Of course not. Just for the joy of it, or for reasons unknown to us, the Lord may equip any one of us supernaturally for an impossible mission. Or he may decide to bypass normal channels, and to reveal his purpose through a miracle. He can show you things about yourself you may never have discovered. He can give you

---

[115] Numbers 21:21-35.

skills you never dreamed of possessing. Who would inhibit God? The Father will do whatever he wants to do!

Nonetheless, do not sit around endlessly waiting for some divine word when common sense tells you what Providence has already fitted you to do.

GOD HONOURS SKILL

Perhaps you have heard a pious teacher say something like this: "Because God wants to improve the display of his glory in you, he will probably call you to a task for which you have neither aptitude nor liking. When the job is done well, despite your bumbling incompetence, God will get greater praise."

How implausible! Believe rather that the Lord will give you a task to match both your skill and desire.

Brush away also superstitious warnings about never telling God what you don't want to do, or where you don't want to go. Foolish people imagine the Father is waiting with vindictive harshness to force them into whatever they declare unpleasant. Far more likely, he will create in you a joyful wish to do what he wants you to do, and give you a sweet yearning to go where he wants you to go.

The Bible gives high honor to skilled people who do their work well;[116] it has little patience with people who arrogate to themselves a role for which God has neither fitted nor chosen them.

---

[116] Such as Bezalel and his fellow craftsmen (Exodus 31:1-1-6; 35:30-36:1); the artisans of David (1 Chronicles 28:21); the warriors of Israel (5:18); and among the temple musicians, Kenaniah (15:22), Asaph and his friends and relatives (25:6,7); Jahath and his colleagues (2 Chronicles 34:12) - along with many others who fitted themselves to serve God by diligently improving their innate skills.

In his provocative book "Addicted to Mediocrity", Franky Schaeffer wrote

> *"each of us has a responsibility to God to exercise our own talents in his or her particular area. There is no blueprint for our life. God does not have a `wonderful plan for your life,' in the sense that there is a spiritual blueprint he will unroll for you.*
>
> *"He deals with each one of us as individuals, where we are. He has given us the talents we have. God is not a dilettante game-player, who gives us one set of talents and then somehow makes us justify our spiritual lives by calling us to give them up. Each person is an individual. Either the whole man is redeemed by Christ or none of him! Christianity is sensible and down to earth, not some spiritual, `Spiritfilled' game!"*[117]

Here then is good sense: begin now to serve God in a way that conforms with who you are, what you are, and where you are. Once you are on the move, if the Father has a different direction for you to go, he can easily show it to you. Meanwhile, you are free to make your own decision about how and where you should serve Christ - both in the world and in the church.

Scripture gives scant reason to think the Lord has only one permissible place for you to live, or one allowable church to join, or one valid career to pursue. On the contrary, many references show how improbable such restricted options would be -

---

[117] Crossway Books, Westchester, Illinois, 1984; pg. 54.

ONLY ONE TOWN?

Luke 10:1-11 tells the story of Jesus sending out thirty-six couples[118] to preach ahead of him, through the entire region. They were to go into all the towns and villages Jesus himself planned to visit later. Notice how Christ gave them only a broad commission, then left the detailed planning to them. How were they to do that? Did Jesus oblige them to pray for divine guidance before they chose which town to enter? No. Did he say: *"Today you must be in this town, and no other, otherwise you will violate God's will!* No. Providing they kept within his plan to preach in every population centre, Jesus gave the disciples freedom to build their own strategy, and to set their own timetable.

Notice also, Christ gave those couples no assurance they would always be successful. On the contrary, he warned them to be ready for failure. Do you realize how strange that warning would be if the Lord had expected them to obtain daily supernatural guidance? How can you fail if the Father himself tells you each day where to go and what to do? After all, the whole purpose of "getting a word from God" is to avoid failure! Fear of failure is the prime impulse of those who refuse to act until God has spoken.

Yet see how terrible it is, this self-imposed burden of invariable success! What bondage it causes. Who can live with such a relentless demand? Who can endure such unyielding pressure? Nothing in life or scripture gives us any warrant to suppose that failure is always avoidable. One of three things happens to those who insist upon

---

[118] Some translations show 35 couples. The manuscript evidence is inconclusive, but for several reasons, 36 couples (that is, 72 disciples) seems the more likely number.

unbroken triumph, who refuse the possibility of defeat:

- an *accumulating* weight of unfulfilled expectations will crush them; or
- they set goals so low, so easy of accomplishment, no honor remains in attaining them; or
- they become so addicted to success they readily abandon the principles of the kingdom of God to achieve it. Adopting secular models, they compromise the true character of the gospel. Many "successful" churches and organizations fall under this indictment. They may be religious bodies; it is doubtful if they are still truly Christian.

All those pathways, and others like them, are witless. Let us work to succeed; but be humble enough to admit that sometimes God chooses to bring greater beauty out of defeat than out of victory.

Thus Christ was pragmatic; if a town would not receive the disciples, he said, they were to "shake even its dust off their feet" and go on to another place. To him it was just as foolish to continue doggedly in a fruitless task, in hope of some unpredictable "breakthrough", as it would be for a farmer to take a plough to a field of rocks. Abandon the place, and find a more fruitful field! Go where the harvest is "white"![119]

Someone may protest that turning one's back on every unresponsive community would mean abandoning half the world to the devil. Not so. Where one preacher has failed, another may succeed; and again, a preacher who cannot break through in one place may enjoy wonderful

---

[119] John 4:35.

success in another. So much depends upon temperament, personal skills, background, cultural affinity, and the like. But a preacher, who remains stubbornly and futilely at his post, is only preventing a person more likely to succeed from coming into that town or church.[120]

Suppose, however, that you *never* find a place or a way to achieve the level of success you have hoped for and dreamed of? Then this saying by Grantland Rice[121] becomes appropriate. It may be a cliché, but its importance remains undiminished

> When the One Great Scorer comes to
> write against your name –
> He marks - not that you won or lost
> but how you played the game.

That is the important thing: to play the game well. Leave the issue of it, the declaration of who won or lost, to God.

Think about art for a moment. We Christians are like painters, of which there are two kinds: those whose primary goal is to make money; and those who cling at any cost to their artistic integrity.[122] The paintings of

---

[120] I remember reading, when I was a teenager, about a missionary who had remained some twenty years on the field, and had won to Christ only a handful of people. He was presented as an example of dauntless heroism, an opinion I agreed with at the time. Now I would simply judge him stubborn. He had accomplished nothing: no school, no hospital, no scripture translation. Just a small group of converts, too few even to comprise a viable church. What a waste of precious years and resources! If he had moved away to a more fruitful field, someone else could have taken his place who may well have reaped a great harvest of souls. As it was, his ill-conceived persistence perhaps prevented a fine church from being established in that town. Only God knows, of course, what might have happened; but it surely remains foolish to keep plowing dead soil (compare Luke 13:6-9).
[121] 1880-1954; from Alumnus Football.
[122] I am not implying that every financially successful artist has behaved dishonorably. Some are fortunate enough to be talented in a style that pleases the public. They can be

Vincent Van Gogh, for example, now sell for many millions; yet in his lifetime his work was scorned, and he sold only one picture to his brother.[123] We all admire the starving artist in his garret, who prefers death to any compromise of his genius - but. few of us are eager to emulate him!

Nonetheless, a true artist is willing to labor at his art, pouring his very soul into it, never sure whether his creations will be revered or reviled. This is indeed -

> Art's long hazard, where no man may choose
> Whether he play to win, or toil to lose.[124]

Every Christian who is striving to make his or her life a work of divine art must dwell with the same uncertainty. Some have been gifted by God in a way that enables them without compromise to gain not only *heaven's* honor but also *earthly* plaudits. Others are not so fortunate. The more nearly they hew their lives to the image God has ordained, the more rejection they suffer from society.

But whether we gain praise or scorn from our neighbors, let us all still strive to create an authentic expression of the special beauty of Christ we have each received. Let us be keepers of the gift of God, artists of integrity, not mere merchants of religion. Just play the game well! Winning or losing in this world is not important!

---

wholly true to their art, and still get rich. I am referring rather to an artist hungry enough for money to compromise his skill, his true genius, by painting below his potential. Too many Christians are like the latter.

[123] Van Gogh (1853-1890), was a Dutch post-impressionist painter. Today "his works are perhaps better known generally than those of any other painter." Columbia Encyclopedia). Suffering from epileptoid seizures, shattered by the rejection of his work, he committed suicide. Recently, one of his paintings was sold for an undisclosed sum, but thought to be above $100 million.

[124] From Caput Mortuum, by Edwin Arlington Robinson (1869-1935).

Discovery

Do Christian tennis players and golfers always win their games? Is the football team from a Christian college guaranteed unbroken success, or even a place among the top teams? Can every Christian artist paint gloriously, or every Christian writer sell a million copies?

How silly! Few will ever achieve renown. Mediocrity inescapably confines most people; they are average men and women with average skills. Though they toil day and night, they will always remain unable to scale the heights of brilliance. In the game of life some win more rounds than others; but not even the best can win all the time without cheating!

Therefore Jesus offered no certainty of continual success. He knew those seventy two disciples would sometimes pick the wrong town; sometimes their preaching would be ineffective. So he prepared them not only for joy, but also for disappointment.

Let us bring those preachers into the twentieth century. We can imagine their despair when they are thrown out of a town without winning a single soul to Christ! We can hear them crying: *"Where did we go wrong? How did we miss the leading of God? If only we had sought more earnestly for divine guidance! Then we would not have come to this town, but to another, where our ministry would have been fruitful!"* We see them, humiliated and ashamed, pleading with the Lord for another chance, promising never again to go anywhere until he tells them to move!

Happily, the disciples were not so fatuous. They saw providence more clearly. They understood that life, like God's earth, is a mixture of mountains and valleys, barren deserts and fertile fields. Those who aspire to the sun-bathed peak must begin in the shadowed vale, and the way to each new crest plunges first into a gloomy chasm. Would you rejoice in the flower-decked meadow? You must also traverse a parched wilderness. Every fragrant garden has its dump of weeds.

WHEN JESUS FAILED

Nobody, not even Jesus, has ever in this world been told they can win every game. Not even Jesus? That's right see *Mark 6:1-6,* which describes a visit Jesus made to his home town. He preached there with little result -

> *"Because of their unbelief, he was not able to do any great miracles in that place, except he made a few sick people well by placing his hands upon them."*

Look at Mark's extraordinary daring. Within the same narrative he tells two stories:

first, how Jesus "failed"; second, how the disciples "succeeded" (vs. 7-13). At least, that is how it appears at first sight: the disciples enjoyed a great Holy Ghost revival; but Christ had to leave town in some disgrace!

Let us create another fanciful portrait. Suppose now that Jesus is a modern preacher, attending a minister's convention. What is his reaction when the delegates compare notes? He hears their glowing reports. They tell of signs, wonders, and miracles! Great crowds! Incredible harvests! Then one of them, an evangelist, asks Jesus, "What happened during your recent crusade in Nazareth?" Jesus looks embarrassed. What can he say? At

Discovery

best, a few sick people were cured. It was a sorry outcome for a man who claims to be sent by God and to possess the power of the Holy Spirit in limitless measure!

Even worse, Jesus rushes to his own defense, adamantly refusing to admit any personal fault. Bluntly, he condemns the people of Nazareth: his crusade had failed, he says, because of *"their* unbelief". The other preachers are aghast. How about a little humility here? Why doesn't this young Galilean acknowledge his own unbelief? Shouldn't he concede some defect in his technique? Doesn't he realize that with proper publicity, better organization, a little tailoring of the message to suit the need of the community, any crusade can be turned from disaster to success? Jesus breaks under their blows. He berates himself. Yes, he was wrong. He should have gathered more prayer-partners; he shouldn't have been so provocative in his message; he should have sought the backing of more religious and civic leaders. He begs the others to pray for him. He asks them to explain the secrets of their success, and he promises to do better next time. Everybody goes home feeling good about themselves.

How preposterous! Yet are we not equally farcical in our attitudes toward life and Christian service? Take the name of Christ out of that illustration, substitute another preacher, and too many people it would all seem quite proper.

Jesus obviously did not think he had "failed", nor did his disciples. Nor did Mark, for he tells how later they all went across the lake to Gennesaret, where they enjoyed stunning "success" – great crowds flocked to hear Christ, and thousands of people found healing simply by touching the edge of his cloak.[125]

AN HONEST EVALUATION

Here is the lesson: if Mark had held some modern ideas about guidance and success, he could never have placed the story of Jesus' apparent failure right alongside an account of the disciple's triumph. The contrast would have been too embarrassing. Mark obviously was not disturbed; therefore he did not share our warped prejudice The moral? We need to redefine "success" and "failure". A good place to begin is Jesus' saying about how little we are worth -

> *"Even if you have done everything you were told to do, you should still say to yourselves, 'we don't deserve any praise, for we have only done our duty!"*[126]

Since none of us have done even so much as our "duty", we have not the slightest claim on God's favor. Whatever we receive from him is purely a gift of his grace in Christ. In the end, the greatest (so-called) of our good works, our ministry achievements, our "successes", are dust blowing in the wind. We should work, of course, work hard, and work well;[127] but remember that apart from the Lord's kindness we are nothing and our work is nothing. The difference between the most famous and the most obscure is only a few years. Give enough time and nobody will know or care whether any one of us lived or died, except God. And what he will care about on that day is not what

---

[125] Mark 6:53-56.
[126] Luke 17:10.
[127] John 9:4; 1 Corinthians 15:10; etc.

you did but *who you were* - that is, your character, not your achievements.

> The surging sea of human life forever onward rolls,
> And bears to the eternal shore its daily freight of souls;
> Though bravely sails our bark today, pale Death sits at the prow, And few will know we ever lived a hundred years from now.
>
> Why prize so much the world's applause? Why dread so much its blame?
> A fleeting echo is its voice of censure or of fame;
> The praise that fills the heart, the scorn that dyes with shame the brow,
> Will be as long-forgotten dreams a hundred years from now.
>
> Our Father to whose sleepless eye the past and future stand
> An open page, like babes we cling to thy protecting hand;
> Change, sorrow, death, are naught to us, if we may safely bow
> Beneath the shadow of thy throne a hundred years from now.[128]

The things you do are important finally only for two things: what they show about your obedience to the call of Christ; what they reveal about the kind of person you are. God will measure, not your works, but *why* you did them,

---

[128] A Hundred Years From Now, stanzas 1,4,8, by Mary A. Ford; date unknown to me, but at least 60 years ago.

how you did them, *who* benefited from them, and *where* you focused the honor of them - upon yourself or Christ.

But now back to the main theme. I hope you realize the significance of Luke's story about Jesus sending out those 36 couples: it offers no grounds for expecting constant, immediate, and sure guidance from God. Instead, it shows the disciples working out their own tactics within the Lord's larger strategy. That is, they were called to preach, and were given parameters inside which they had to work; but the boundaries were wide, and within them the disciples were free to make personal choices day by day. Sometimes those decisions led to joyous success, sometimes to bitter disappointment. It did not matter. Whatever the result, they were in harmony with the purpose of God.

BROUGHT INTO PARTNERSHIP

In the same passage of scripture[129] there is a startling insight into the kind of relationship the Father wants to establish with us. What is that relationship? Master and slaves? Puppeteer and puppets? Employer and employees? None of those. Rather, he invites us into a breathtaking *partnership* with him. Does the harvest field need more workers? Then, said 3esus, we share a burden with the Father to send out reapers!

Hardly any passage of scripture shows more clearly the nobility God has conferred upon us in Christ. What dignity! What awesome responsibility! What privilege! How marvelous his kindness! God invites you, urges you, to stand tall in his grace, as his friend and associate. He

---
[129] Luke 10:1-2.

wants no wooden marionettes dancing on the end of a divine string. He wants real men and women working with him to fulfill their true destiny and his highest glory.

The command to *"pray for more reapers"* implies the flexibility of the plan of God; it shows that he is willing to conform to our desires, just as we are required to surrender to his purpose. The same command refutes the idea that God has already drawn up a daily roster for your life. Discard the notion that you have to drag a pre-printed timetable out of God's reluctant hand, and then follow its schedule minutely. That may be the duty of serfs; it hardly applies to partners! We are not obliged, like those in chains, to give blind obedience to unexplained commands.

A REDEMPTIVE POWER

How can God grant us such astonishing liberty? Suppose, for example, that Paul was wrong when he insisted (against strong warnings) on going to Jerusalem, willing, even eager, to die for Christ?[130] What about all the churches he might have built, all the souls he might have saved, if instead of lying confined in Caesar's prison he had been actively preaching Christ? Does God really give us license to be mistaken?

Yes, we do have such broad liberty - to succeed and to fail, to be wise or foolish, to prosper or to be made poor. Why? Because in the end it doesn't matter. God's concerns are not statistical. He works on character, not arithmetic. He does not measure success by numbers, but by personal

---

[130] Acts 20:22-24; 21:4,10-14. This incident is discussed in greater detail in the next chapter.

quality. Once again, his appraisal is not based upon what you *do,* but on who you *are.*

Beyond that again, remember this: he is *God* - the One who *"works all things together for the good of those who love him."*[131] W who believe can never be defeated; for us there is no final failure. What the devil, the flesh, the world, meant for our ruin God turns to our salvation. He works in every event to give it a redemptive purpose. You may have wrought wonderfully or woefully; in either case the Lord will bring out of your life - if you trust him - his larger purpose and fit you to inherit his glory![132]

We should learn to be equally suspicious of both prosperity and poverty. Rudyard Kipling showed his understanding of this when he wrote his great poem, *If -*

> If you can dream - and not make dreams your master;
> If you can think - and not make thoughts your aim;
> If you can meet with triumph and disaster
> And treat those two impostors just the same
> You'll be a man my son![133]

Said the poet, there are two great impostors: *triumph* and *distaste.*[134] You can turn either one of them into a

---

[131] Romans 8:28.

[132] Of course, it is understood that you have not deliberately perverted the will of God, nor acted against scripture. Yet even in such cases, if there is true repentance and a renewed desire to serve the Lord well, he is able to "restore the years the locusts have eaten" (Joel 2:12-14, 18-19, 25-26).

[133] I have quoted the first few lines of the second stanza, plus the last line of the poem.

[134] No power or want of skill could have led Nature into the error of allowing good and evil to be visited indiscriminately on the virtuous and the sinful alike. Yet living and dying, honor and dishonor, pain and pleasure, riches and poverty, and so forth, are

stairway to heaven, or a steep slide into hell. The choice is yours. Better still; learn to treat them both with equal disdain. Like Paul, we should discover in Christ how to keep a calm spirit, whether we have gained everything or lost everything![135] Like Alfred the Great (in Winston Churchill's fine phrase), the wise man or woman will "greet returning fortune with a cool eye"[136] -for what was won yesterday may be lost today; what was lost today, may be won again tomorrow! Who knows what the day will bring?

One of the proverbs states this clearly -

> "We devise many plans in our hearts; but the purpose of the Lord prevails over them all"[137]

You seldom see him, hear him, or feel him; but without resting, the Lord is ever at work. Silently he answers prayer, shapes results, opens or closes doors. Constantly he is forming or transforming all things, so that nothing less than his complete will is done. Note, though, how the proverb still establishes your freedom (and mine) *"to devise your own plans"*. We do have that right; but God

---

equally the lot of good men and bad. Things like these neither elevate nor degrade; and therefore they are no more good than they are evil." (Book Two, #11; tr. by Maxwell Staniforth; Penguin Books, 1986; pg. 48.)

[135] Philippians 4:12.

[136] History of the English-Speaking Peoples, Vol 1, Ch. 7. The phrase is part of a majestic portrayal Churchill gives of the king: "This sublime power to rise above the whole force of circumstances, to remain unbiased by the extremes of victory or defeat, to persevere in the teeth of Continued from page 93... disaster, to greet returning fortune with a cool eye, to have faith in men after repeated betrayals, raises Alfred far above the turmoil of barbaric wars to his pinnacle of deathless glory." Alfred was a devout man, who deeply feared God, and accepted the task of preserving England as a Christian country against the pagan Viking invaders. Churchill's sonorous description provides a model of Christian character we would all do well to emulate.

[137] Proverbs (19:21)

has a greater right. No matter what plans we implement, the Lord exerts sovereignty over them, and brings out of them whatever he pleases. As Plato once said -

> *"God governs all things, and ... chance and opportunity co-operate with him in the government of human affairs".*[138]

This happening or that may be mere chance, an unplanned opportunity, nothing more than the outworking of daily cause and effect. Is the Sovereign Lord taken by surprise? Is his rule baffled, his purpose thwarted? No, he laughs in the heavens and imposes his will upon earth![139] The wrath of empires turns to his glory, the rage of hell builds his kingdom. All things are compelled to fulfill his desire.

PASSIVE OR ACTIVE?

Can I say it again? The scriptures we have looked at so far, and the ideas we have considered, leave no place for fatalism in Christian thinking. We are not automatons, jerking in response to a predetermined future. On the contrary, the future for us remains open-ended, susceptible to our influence. William Henley, in his defiant poem *"Invictus"*, was not altogether wrong when he wrote:

> It matters not how strait the gate,
> How charged with punishment the scroll,
> I am the master of my fate;

---

[138] I do not have the source of this quote; except that I think it comes from his "Laws".
[139] Psalm 2:1-6.

> I am the captain of my soul.[140]

There is an almost terrifying truth in those lines. Without realizing it, the poet was trying to seize an independence that already belonged to him: an astonishing God-given right to determine his own destiny. God has never removed that right; it lies now at your disposal. Some choose to use this liberty to rebel against the holy purpose of the Lord; others, to serve their God with joy. But the privilege remains. We should strive to employ it responsibly and intelligently. Don't abdicate your authority by making God responsible for every decision you face. The Father does not want a shelf of puppets. He desires a family of ever-growing and ever more trustworthy children.

---

[140] W. E. Henley, English poet, 1849-1903. "Invictus" begins with the words, "Out of the night that covers me ... " Dorothea Day (of whom I know nothing more than her name) wrote a rejoinder poem, which begins, "Out of the light that dazzles me ... ", and goes on to match Henley line by line with an affirmation, not of defiant despair, but of joyful faith.

Alison's Story

WE MOVE TO TASMANIA (1963-1978)

After five years in Adelaide we decided to move to Launceston in Tasmania, once again following the call in answer to a need! There was a small church in Launceston, needing a pastor, and we were ready to go. We did not know it at the time, but here God would teach us some vital lessons in faith, and by assimilating those lessons we would gain two miracle sons!

After we had been in Tasmania for some time I began to feel the urge to become a mother again. It was an enormously strong desire, and we began to pray about it. On the surface it seemed madness to attempt another pregnancy. I had spent so much time in bed, and had suffered so much to have Sharon, and now had two children to look after as well as a busy church schedule.

But I did become pregnant again, only to lose yet another child, once again at two months.

This time the doctor told me that from now on all my babies would terminate at two months. I had too many antibodies to bear a child, and in those days no one knew how to overcome this problem.

Ken and I spent some time talking this over. How could we continue to preach that Jesus was the healer if we could not have any more babies? If I hadn't wanted a baby there would be no problem; but I did! The God who gave me the yearning to have more children, and who allowed me to become pregnant, surely could work a miracle and help me to overcome this difficulty in my body.

I reasoned this way. If God didn't want me to have any more babies, all he would have to do would be to close up my womb as he had with Rachel in Old Testament times. Since he hadn't done that, but had allowed me to get pregnant, to me was sure proof he would help me. He who had given me the desire for motherhood would also give me the baby I wanted so much.

Despite these rationalizations, I wasn't going to rush in and conceive again without a definite word from God. Not only was there a strong probability of another miscarriage, but now (said the obstetrician) my own life was at risk. I might die myself if I tried to have another baby! What I needed was the faith of God, an unwavering certainty that he was with me, and that I had nothing to fear in attempting another pregnancy.

Finally after much prayer I said to Ken, "If I discover another couple who have had a similar problem, and it is established that God intervened in their life, granting them a baby, then I will go ahead."

We continued to pray. Some time passed. One day in the mail we received a magazine from the USA. In it was this testimony from an American physician, Dr Wilham Standish-Reed:

QUESTION: My wife and I have an RH incompatibility. As a result, my wife has lost her last two children by miscarriages. Do you believe that we can hope to have children? Or should my wife or I have an operation to prevent any further conception?

ANSWER: A very dear friend of mine, a minister, at one time had this same problem. When his wife again conceived they faced long months of anxiety, wondering whether they would have a normal child, or even if she would be able to carry the pregnancy through to its entirety. At that time I had been studying the church's ministry of healing. I advised the minister to lay hands on his wife daily, and pray in the name of Jesus of Nazareth, asking God to allow her to have a normal pregnancy and a normal child. ... It is my feeling that a pregnancy carried through with husband and wife praying together would produce wonderful results. The minister's wife had a normal child. Only God knows how he could "juggle the genes" to cause such a result.

We were overjoyed! Here was the guidance for which we had been asking. We set ourselves to pray for each other. Every night Ken laid his hands on me and prayed for me; then I would pray for him. This seemed so right to us. God had answered our prayer and given us specific instructions through a medical doctor, which gave us the extra confidence we needed. For us, it was like another verse added to the Bible; a promise of healing with our names on it! God would do for us what he had done for others!

After some months I became aware that I had conceived again. I was excited, though a little apprehensive. I rang my doctor and she was horrified, despite my assurance to her that this time all would be well. She examined me, and to my astonishment told me that I was already three months pregnant. She took some blood from me and had it tested. I still had my antibodies but they were not harming the baby. She took some of Ken's blood, it had not changed.

In fact, nothing had changed! Except that against all probability I was having a successful pregnancy, with no sign of losing the baby! She kept asking me what we had done, and I kept telling her that we had prayed about it, and God was giving us a miracle baby.

She was a Christian doctor, so she had to accept what was happening; even though, as far as she knew at that time, it was not possible. Later on we were to discover that God had intervened to "juggle our genes" and to give us an Rh-negative baby.

In due time, and without being obliged to spend even one day in bed, I gave birth to our second son, Eric, who is now 25 years of age, and happily married to Julie. Together they have given us two delightful granddaughters!

While in hospital I spoke to my pediatrician, who was caring for Eric, and I asked him, 'Doctor, do you understand how this could have happened?"

He admitted that he did not know, but he did give me a warning. "This was a one in a million chance. Don't try to do it again. It won't work another time."

God must have heard him and decided to do it again! Four years later our third son, Baden, was born. He is now 20 years of age and is a joy to us and a constant reminder that God can repeat his miracles whenever he pleases!

Now we were able to rejoice in our God who does all things well. Ken began to pray for others who had a desperate longing to bear children, but who for some reason were unable to conceive. There are many such testimonies, but the one I will share with you happened in Perth, Western Australia. Ken was preaching in a church there and had a sudden insight, a "word of knowledge", that there were two women in the congregation who wanted a child but were unable to conceive. Two young ladies came forward, weeping; one had been married six years, and the other eight years. God had cared for them enough to reveal their deep longing to a visiting preacher!

Ken prayed for them and then left Perth to return home. Ten months later we received a letter from their pastor. They had both had baby girls One after nine months and one week, and the other after nine months and two weeks!

Why was God teaching us such mighty lessons of faith? Looking back, we can see that God was growing a teacher! It takes perhaps only five or ten minutes to grow an evangelist. Anyone who has been saved can become a soul-winner, burning to tell others about Jesus; but it takes God 20 years to prepare a teacher!

Sixth Fallacy

I CAN MARRY ONLY THE SPOUSE GOD HAS CHOSEN"

King Canute was one of the greatest monarchs in England's history. He flourished during the first part of the 11th century, and at the peak of his power was sovereign over six realms, in England and on the Continent. So impressed were his flattering courtiers by his wise laws, and apparently invincible power, they began to say that nothing was impossible for him. Surely even the mighty waves would turn back at his command! Such extravagant praise vexed the modest and devout Canute, so he determined to shame those fawners. He bade them place a chair on the English south coast, near Southampton, upon which he sat, as on a throne, while he ordered the tide to retreat. The waves ignored him, and rolled relentlessly on, until the incoming water began to wash over his feet. Then the king rebuked his attendants: "See how feeble is the power of men and of kings. Not even the smallest of these ripples heed my word!"

If a little more of that modesty and humility had possessed some Christians I know, they would have saved themselves much pain and high embarrassment. Unlike Canute, they thought they *could* turn back the tide and command the seas to do their will! How astonished they were when events rolled heedlessly on, and they barely escaped being drowned in the careless flood! It is good for us to recognize our limitations, to accept what cannot be changed, to keep our pretensions within the bounds of scripture.

This chapter looks at divine guidance through two different examples. Both of them show the need for realism, humility, and practical sense as you go about learning and living the will of God. The first deals with the issue of choosing a spouse; the second shows how Paul worked out the will of God in his own life.

CHOOSING A SPOUSE

"You have asked me about those among you who are unmarried. The Lord has not given me any specific command; but here is my personal opinion – which I hope you will respect because of the grace God has given me. You know that a time of persecution is coming, so it is probably best for everyone to stay as they are. If you are married, don't get divorced; if you are single, don't get married. However, if a young man and a young woman choose to marry, they will not be doing anything wrong. But they will bring upon themselves many troubles, and I am trying to spare you unnecessary grief...

"If a man finds that he cannot control his behavior with his betrothed, because his passions are too urgent, then let him have his way and marry her. If it must be, then it must be! It is no sin to marry. But if a man, strong in character and resolute in purpose,

who is able to keep his desires in check, makes up his mind not to marry his betrothed, he too should be approved. So, those who marry do well; but those who do not marry do even better."

"A wife is bound to her husband for as long as he is alive. But if he dies, she is free to marry any man she wishes, providing he is a Christian – although in my opinion (which I think comes from the Spirit of God) she will be happier if she remains a window."[141]

What decision has more important consequences than the choice of a spouse? Yet Paul fails even to suggest that the unmarried should earnestly seek divine guidance before deciding whether or not to marry, or who their spouse should be. Simply and bluntly he says: "You can marry anyone you please, providing he or she is a Christian."

Search the passage; you will not find a hint that the men and women in Corinth (whether married or single) should ask God to tell them what to do.

Paul in fact based all his counsel on practical considerations: the troubles married couples will experience; the different levels of self-control people have; the needs of other people; and the like. He gave his opinion on these matters, and reckoned his thoughts were shaped by the Holy Spirit - but he disavowed any specific command from God. Those who marry, he says with some pessimism, "will face many troubles"; *but they are not sinning. They are free to sustain whatever state they please, celibate or conjugal. They had no need of a special*

---
[141] 1 Corinthians 7:25-28, 36-40.

"word" from God; they were capable of acting wisely by themselves.

In the end, Paul did nothing more than explain the options, lay down some guidelines, and then leave the people free to make their choice. If special help is not usually available for such a vital concern as matrimony, why be surprised if it is lacking for many lesser decisions we have to make?

A TROUBLE-FREE LIFE?

Did you notice the phrase "many troubles"? Expressions like that, which occur often in Paul's writings, tell us he did not embrace what people sometimes call the "faith message"[142]. He neither taught nor expected that "the right kind of faith" would bring to any "believer" immunity from trouble and unalloyed prosperity. Some "faith" preachers have tried to surmount this difficulty by accusing Paul of lacking a full "revelation" in the word. "If Paul had known what we know," they claim with astounding impudence, "he could have escaped the hurts he suffered." I find Paul's testimony (2 Corinthians 11:23 - 12:10) more moving than theirs.

ASTONISHING FLEXIBILITY

How distant Paul was also from the pious legalists who yearn to hammer every Christian into the same mould! How flexible he was in his approach! See how he acknowledges the variety that exists among people: one

---

[142] I do not mean that Paul was not a preacher of faith, which he most surely was. No man save Jesus has ever had a better revelation in the word of God, or such unwavering trust in the divine promises. I think of myself, too, as a "faith" preacher - but I dislike the extreme versions of the "faith" message, and the distortions of it, that some have embraced.

man, he says, cannot endure an unmarried state; another can handle celibacy with ease.[143] For the former, the pressures and temptations are too great - he is under "compulsion" - *so the sensible thing for him to do is to marry as soon as he can! But the latter has his urges under stern control. He tolerates, even enjoys, a virtuous single life. For him, to remain unmarried is no burden; therefore let him remain a bachelor, so that he may serve the Lord better.*

It is hard to imagine some modern preachers talking like that. They scour scripture for a magical key to spiritual victory, then impose it upon everyone. They offer a single formula to provide the same level of self-control for every Christian. No one is different, they say; the gospel works identically for every man and woman. If one person can remain happily celibate, then all can. If one couple can remain happily married, then all can. Every believer (they say) should know continuing prosperity; they should all be free of sickness, never in need of healing. Every Christian should have the same measure of joy, the same unwavering hope, the same sure confidence.

What monotonous conformity! Happily, the Lord will have none of it. He has made us all dissimilar. What is easy for one may be a huge struggle, or even impossible for another. Where one soars upward, another can barely walk.

We need to back away from being our brother's conscience. We need to allow each other the latitude written in scripture. Why should I tell you what to eat, drink, or wear, or how you should live? Who gave you the

---

[143] Verses 35-37.

right to tell me? You and I should bravely declare the *moral strictures* of scripture; but beyond that, let each person decide for himself or herself how best to serve the Lord.[144]

SOBER ANALYSIS

Notice how little of supernatural guidance lies in the expressions Paul uses. He talks about a man who decides to remain unmarried, and says that this man

> *"has settled the matter in his mind ... is not driven by any uncontrollable urge ... governs his will ... has made up his mind ... does the right thing."*

Those phrases all imply personal volition, not divine control. The picture is not one of a man who is asking heaven to solve his quandary. Rather, we see a man who has carefully thought about the issues, measured his strengths and weaknesses, and then made a responsible decision. In this case, not to marry. But a different man might just as well have decided the opposite. Neither decision would have been spiritually or morally wrong.

Nor does Paul offer any suggestion that the man who had trouble subduing his natural urges could get everything under control if only he would exercise more faith, or speak out the promise more boldly, or walk in the Spirit more fervently. The apostle was not troubled by the fact that people are strong in one thing and weak in another, nor because they differ immensely from each other in

---

[144] For more insight into this principle, read Romans 14:1-22. Notice also how Jesus acknowledged that for some people either a celibate or a married state might be intolerable, Matthew 19:10-11; and cp. also 1 Corinthians 7:7-9.

their capabilities. He allowed them to be themselves and to pursue the path that was right for each of them in God.

MAKE UP YOUR MIND

Paul gives an unmarried woman the same license;[145] except that she (like the man) may only marry a Christian. Paul probably based this instruction on Numbers 36:6, which tells how Moses gave a group of Israeli maidens' liberty to marry whom they would, but only within the tribe. Notice again, neither the great lawgiver nor the apostle ever suggests that marriage cannot be entered until God has specifically identified one's future spouse. The woman, says Paul, "is free to marry anyone she chooses." *Her husband does not have to be a man supernaturally directed to her by the Lord. He need only be a Christian.*

A wise woman, of course, will look for more in a husband than just a profession of faith in Christ. She ought to choose a spouse who is manly, kind, strong, patient, hardworking, respectful of her, dedicated to the church. But she hardly needs God's help to find such a man. Common sense is adequate!

Someone might object: "What about Proverbs 19:14, which says that 'a good wife is a gift from the Lord'?" *(see also 18:22)*

The idea is not that this "good wife" is a personal gift from God, but more that of Proverbs 3:6 - "In all your ways acknowledge God, and he will direct your paths." *Or, she is a gift of God in the same sense that a rich harvest is God's gift. True, there will be no harvest apart from God's*

---

[145] Verse 39.

providence. Nonetheless, any farmer who waits for a miracle of heaven to plant his seed, fertilize his fields, and reap his crops, will soon starve to death. There is work for the farmer to do, with wisdom and diligence. Then his fields will flourish under the favor of God!

Neither should a man seeking a wife, nor a woman a husband, sit at home praying for the Lord to make it happen. Let them instead follow Paul's sage counsel, and think about the matter themselves, carefully and honestly.

Do you want to marry? Then decide the kind of spouse you ought to be yourself, and the kind of spouse you need to wed. Act cautiously and prudently. Physical attraction alone is a poor reason for undertaking marriage. Just as important, if not more so, are such issues as: Christian dedication, spiritual maturity, cultural background, intellectual equality, social status, recreational preferences, fiscal policies, child-rearing ideas, and the like. All these should be considered, and frankly discussed, before you say "yes" to any prospective spouse.

Given that kind of responsible attitude, a sensible man really will not need God's help, nor will a sensible woman, to find a suitable mate. Those pragmatic people probably will ask the Lord to keep them from rushing into folly. They might ask him also to teach them wisdom. Nor would it hurt to seek his help in meeting some eligible and godly suitors, from among whom a wise choice can be made.

Nevertheless, the burden of choosing a good spouse still belongs to us more than to God. That is the measure of the freedom the Lord has given us to shape our own lives.

Will you use that liberty wisely or foolishly? Will you allow your choices to be formed by scripture or by secular philosophy? Will you strive toward God's purpose or worldly ambition? Will your ruling principle be love or self-interest? Those are the important questions.

A REAL CYNIC!

Solomon once made a cynical comment on choosing a spouse. He had no doubt that the value to a man of a devoted and capable woman was far above rubies. But he thought it unlikely that a true paragon of wifely virtues would ever come his way.[146] *"One man among a thousand I have found,"* he sighed, *"but a woman among these I have yet to find!"*[147] And if a man should happen to find a true woman, it was more by good fortune than good management!

Should we agree with Solomon? No, because we Christians have advantages Solomon lacked. We have more of the wisdom of God, more of the mind of Christ, more of the subtly guiding hand of the Holy Spirit. It is not difficult for Christian men and women to choose wisely, to marry well, and to build godly and pleasant homes.

Nearly four decades ago I found just such a precious jewel as Solomon describes, a woman who still fills me with wonder and joy, my wife Alison. Why are others not so fortunate? Not because of a lack of options, as the skeptic king thought, but mostly because of failure to behave circumspectly. I have seen many marriages based on a so-called "leading" from God collapse in bitterness. I have

---

[146] Proverbs 31:10, ff.
[147] Ecclesiastes 7:28.

seldom seen an unhappy marriage that began with good sense and careful choice.

Solomon may have been cynical, but he was nonetheless sensible. The idea that one's mate should be chosen by God never entered his head. Therefore he was pessimistic about the possibility of a happy marriage. For despite what I have just said, no matter how judiciously men and women behave, they may still find themselves in a bad marriage. Scan through Proverbs, and you will find many references to domestic strife. Nowhere will you find it said that such troubles could be avoided if only people would let God pick their spouse. Advice is given on how to find a worthy partner, and on how to build a strong relationship; but no guarantees of success exist. Every Christian has a sure promise of unfailing inward joy; but no one knows if they will enjoy circumstantial happiness.

Paul recognized the same thing: sometimes even a marriage between two godly people does not work. He spoke about a quarrelling couple in his letter to the Corinthians. He wished them to be reconciled. If that were not possible, he allowed them to live apart, or to be legally separated.[148] Paul did not rebuke them for their failure; he did not insist that all they needed was more of the grace of God, or more faith. The apostle knew that sometimes deep and unresolvable hurts develop between two people. The glory of God and human happiness were alike served better by removing from the couple the burden of each other's presence. Both of them could then live in peace and serve the church in freedom.[149]

Over the years I have heard several preachers say

---

[148] 1 Corinthians 7:10-11.
[149] Solomon taught the same thing, albeit more colorfully - Proverbs 21:9; 25:24; 27:15.

accurately that we are like passengers on an ocean liner. We can't get off the ship until it reaches port. So we have to travel in the direction set by the captain. But while on board we are free to utilize in any way we please all the facilities and opportunities the ship provides. Occasionally, too, the captain may invite us to dine at his table; who would be rude enough to refuse?

Similarly, we may say that God has generally mapped out our life's journey, but mostly leaves the details to us. Providing we keep within the wide parameters he has set, we are free to make all kinds of personal decisions. There is no need to keep asking permission from the Master to do one thing or another. He may of course choose at any time to approach us directly, giving this or that command, replacing our plans with his. To surrender to his purpose, to dine at his table when he so commands, is our delight. Otherwise, we are content to get on with fulfilling what each new day requires of us. Let us do so with unhesitating faith and unwavering holiness.

PAUL AND DIVINE GUIDANCE

The uncertainty of miraculous intervention provides another confirmation of the rule we are discussing.[150] For example, on one occasion, within 24 hours of being incarcerated, Paul was liberated from prison by an earthquake.[151] But there were other times when he had to endure imprisonment for long years.[152] When his release finally came, no tangible miracle happened. Was Paul abandoned by God, because no angel or earthquake

---

[150] That God's program for your life and Christian service is flexible, not fixed.
[151] Acts 16:22-26.
[152] Acts 24:27; 28:16,30.

came to break open the prison door? Of course not. Supernatural grace was with him all the time, working sometimes obviously, sometimes unobtrusively. Paul made no complaint. With or without chains he was in the hands of God. When the Lord intervened, he obeyed the heavenly vision. When there was no sight or sound from heaven, he followed his own wisdom. This unpredictability of divine intervention argues against the proposition of constant supernatural guidance. Instead it suggests no more than occasional intervention by God when the divine purpose requires it.

Someone may protest: "Scripture itself shows God leading Paul miraculously. What about the `Macedonian Call'? What about the times when the Holy Spirit stopped Paul from going into Asia, and into Bythinia?"

Those are fair questions, for Luke does tell us how the Holy Spirit acted both negatively and positively when he guided Paul. That is, Paul was both prevented by God from going to some places, and firmly instructed to go to others.[153]

Doesn't this prove we should all expect the same kind of guidance? Hardly. Even for Paul such supernatural direction was unusual, which is why Luke gave special attention to it when it happened. If such obvious guidance were not uncommon, why did Luke describe those few occasions so dramatically?

Even more striking is Paul's reaction. Despite the startling intervention of the Holy Spirit, the apostle allowed only a temporary delay of his plans. Later, after

---

[153] Acts 16:6-10.

he had obeyed the heavenly vision, Paul resumed his original purpose, and went to the very places from which the Spirit had earlier turned him aside. Unless explicit instructions were coming to him from above, he obviously felt free to make and pursue his own plans.

MANY TROUBLES

One passage of high drama shows how infrequently Paul's steps were specifically controlled by God. He lists the shocking array of hardships and cruelty he had suffered: in prison more often than any other apostle; flogged more terribly; constantly threatened by death; torn by the cat five times; beaten with rods three times; nearly killed by a stone-throwing mob; shipwrecked three times; sleepless, starving, cold, naked, exhausted, worn down by the burden of the churches. What a staggering burden of sorrows! Yet Paul is still not done. He continues -

> "... in danger from raging floods,
> in danger from wild robbers,
> in danger from jealous Jews,
> in danger from angry Gentiles,
> in danger from city mobs,
> in danger from parched deserts,
> in danger from ocean hurricanes,
> in danger from bitter Christians!"[154]

What will you say to such things? That God deliberately thrust Paul into beatings, stonings, floggings, and imprisonments? That these horrors were done by the Father's express will? That Paul, having asked the Lord

---

[154] See 2 Corinthians 11:23-28.

to guide him, was then carefully led into shipwrecks, riots, whippings, starvation, and nakedness? Asking the question is enough to expose its folly.

The Father of course knew that Paul's apostolic ministry would bring him into many perils and cause him much suffering.[155] Jesus had predicted the same for all his disciples.[156] To say that hardship and persecution will fall upon the church, however, differs from saying that each outburst of hatred is a product of God's will. What a monster that would make God!

Perhaps some would argue that while God does not arouse persecution, nonetheless he leads his people into it. That seems hardly less monstrous than the other. Better by far to accept the obvious meaning of Paul's statement: when they heard him preach, some people

welcomed him, others despised him; some reached out to him with love, others fell upon him with curses. The Father intervened only when his specific purpose required it: sometimes guiding Paul by a vision, but not usually; sometimes rescuing him by a miracle, but not usually; sometimes providing for him supernaturally, but not usually. Mostly, the apostle's life followed the pattern of those around him, a life governed by conventional laws of cause and effect, which the Father disturbed only occasionally.[157]

---

[155] Acts 9:16.

[156] John 16:2,33; Matthew 10:16-23; 24:9.

[157] Of course, I exempt from this restriction miracles wrought by Paul's own hand: healing the sick, casting out demons, displaying the various gifts of the Holy Spirit, and the like - cp. Romans 15:18-19; Hebrews 2:4; etc. In this sense the apostles were like their Master. The power of God expressed through their ministry was designed more to help others than to help themselves. Divine intervention on their own behalf, to give them extraordinary protection, favor, or guidance, was infrequent, as it is for all of us.

MOVE AHEAD!

So the principle is clear: Paul remained open to a "word" from God, and submissive to the will of God; nonetheless he continued to write his own agenda. He took personal responsibility for how and where and when he would fulfill his apostolic ministry. He was not dependent upon miracles of guidance. The kind of supernaturalism that characterizes many Christians is absent from Paul's story. The great apostle depended more upon his inner wisdom, than he did upon the kind of imported, external, miraculous guidance so many people devote much time and effort to finding.

Here is something else from the same passage: guidance comes out of motion. Paul was advancing when the Spirit gave him further direction. It is difficult to steer a car or a ship when they are stationary! So don't sit around waiting and pleading for some vision. Don't keep listening for some voice. Get out and get busy. The harvest is ready!

David Livingstone once said to a friend -

> *"I think you are not quite clear upon the indications of Providence, my dear brother. I don't think we ought to wait for them. Our duty is to go forward and (then) look for the indications."*[158]

Go forward! expecting great things from God. Go forward! knowing that, seen or unseen, your steps are supervised by the Lord. Go forward! trusting the Father to complete his purpose for your life. Go forward! ready for a miracle if

---

[158] The source of this quote is unknown to me.

nothing less will suffice to do God's will. Go forward!

TAKING PERSONAL RESPONSIBILITY

With obvious sorrow, with unhappy resignation to the unavoidable, Luke describes Paul's stubborn determination to go to Jerusalem. Many prophetic voices had warned the apostle that imprisonment and possibly death awaited him in Judaea. Again and again the Spirit had spoken, culminating in a dramatic message from the prophet Agabus.[159] Always the word was the same: don't go to Jerusalem!

All Paul's companions, including Luke,[160] thought he should have heeded those warnings.[161] Was the apostle wrong? Did he suffer unnecessary imprisonment? Was his ministry needlessly interrupted? Who can say? Perhaps it was perverse of Paul to cling so defiantly to his wish to bear witness for Christ in Jerusalem, perhaps not. Think those many prophecies and warnings would have been enough to make *me* change my mind! Not out of cowardice, but simply prudence. Paul obviously thought otherwise. Indeed, in his heart he was convinced that he had no other choice.[162]

---

[159] Acts 20:22-24, 21:4, 10-14.

[160] Luke is included in the plural pronoun, "we".

[161] Note again Acts 21:4, " ... prompted by the Holy Spirit, they told Paul constantly not to go to Jerusalem."

[162] See Acts 20:22. Some translations read it, "I am compelled by the (Holy) Spirit." Others prefer, "I feel a compulsion in (my own) spirit." The Greek is indeterminate. However, if "pneuma" should be read here as (Holy) Spirit, then there is a peculiar contradiction in the story. Why would the Spirit say one thing through many prophets, but another thing to Paul? So it seems better to make it a reference to Paul's spirit. Nonetheless, that inner desire was so intense it had for Paul the strength of necessity. He felt that he could not resist it. It pushed him like a command from heaven.

Some say God wanted Paul to spend those years in prison, in Caesarea and in Rome, so that he could write his "prison epistles". That is hardly valid, for Paul wrote other letters, just as powerful, while he was in active ministry. So did the other apostles.

What is more significant is this: whether Paul's determination to stick to his plan was foolish or wise, he never doubted that he was free to do what he thought best. *Not even the passionate actions of Agabus were enough to deter him, nor the tears of his friends, nor the pleas of the elders. He had made his decision. He saw no reason to change it. This was his God-given right. It is the same right* you *have.*

The extraordinary autonomy seized by Paul ill fits the pattern of those who refuse to act without some divine "revelation". It sits even less comfortably with those who allow themselves to be fettered by such "revelations"! Paul allowed, indeed wanted, prophets like Agabus to speak. He listened to them with respect. But in the end he permitted no-one to strip away his God-given prerogative to make his own decisions and to walk his own path. Nor should you.

Discovery

Alison's Story

GUIDANCE FROM ACROSS THE PACIFIC! (1974)

The phone rang. It was after midnight and Ken dragged himself reluctantly out of bed. An excited voice came over the wire. It was our good friend Peter Vacca, calling from 600 miles away. He had been praying and had seen a vision of a map of the world with a light glowing in our city of Launceston. As he watched, the light spread all over Australia, then across to New Zealand, and then around the world.

Peter was so impressed and stirred by his vision that he had to ring us and let us know. Could we explain what it meant? Ken and I weren't sure, but we said we would certainly pray about it.

Around this same time, one of the ladies from our church traveled across to Perth, and while there she heard a prophecy that a tree would grow out of Launceston, and its branches would spread over Australia, then across to New Zealand, and on around the world. A remarkably similar prophecy! But some months would pass before we could understand what God was saying to us.

For twelve years we had labored in Tasmania, and through this period God had blessed us with great miracles. Many people had found healing in Jesus' name, our own congregation was growing, and we had helped establish four other churches. They had been years of laughter and tears, sunshine and sadness, happiness and frustration. There had been both defeats and triumphs. Much had been done, but Ken was troubled by a feeling that he had not fulfilled the purpose of God.

I believe the Lord himself caused this, for it made Ken seek God earnestly about what his future should be. God denied him complete satisfaction in local church ministry, because he wanted to draw him into a special path, a hard path, and one that would take great sacrifice.

Ken became sure that God wanted to speak to him, to direct him in some way, and that he would find the answer in the USA. I was not fully aware of all that my husband was going through, but I knew he was struggling and needed encouragement. When he mentioned that he wanted to go to America, I knew at once this was from God. For both of us this was unusual. It was a dramatic departure from our normal way of understanding God's will. Why go to the USA? Couldn't the Lord speak in Australia? Yet we both knew this decision came from God.

Even then, it was only by a series of miracles Ken ever got to America. Perhaps Satan was standing against him, sensing that this was a turning point in our lives. Perhaps the Enemy knew that something would come from this trip that would help in building God's kingdom. So we had to contend with opposition from people, a lost visa that turned up at the last moment on a plane that was not scheduled to fly, a pilot's strike, and many other irritations from the enemy. Or perhaps they were from God, once more testing our faith?

SUPERNATURAL REVELATION

My experience and Ken's in guidance had been fairly uniform until now. When we needed to know God's will we spent some time reviewing the situation and writing down the facts. Then we would make a reasonable decision based on those facts, using scripture and the wisdom God had planted in us over the years.

This time God spoke to Ken so differently that he was not able to accept it fully for a long time, not until it began to come to pass.

When he arrived in the USA, he was ready to give up full-time ministry. He had given the Lord 20 years of his life, and though God had been very gracious and taught him many things, he was deeply dissatisfied, feeling that something vital was lacking from his life. Perhaps it was time to find a new way to serve the Lord?

But what did God want him to do? How would those prophecies about the light and the tree be fulfilled? He was perplexed and unsure, yet still hopeful that during his time in America the Lord would give him insight, and enable him to make a decision. Did God want him to write the books he felt he should write? Did it matter? Was it important to God?

His first stop was a church in Anaheim. He had no sooner sat down and begun to look around him than the Lord electrified him with these words, given by prophecy from the pastor who was leading the meeting that morning -

"There is a preacher here who is thinking of leaving the full-time ministry. If you do that, it will be a very costly mistake. God has called you and still has a work for you to do. The Lord forbids you to go back into secular business."

Since Ken had been contemplating buying a small business in Australia, he had no doubt this warning was directed at him! So here was something different from the usual silent prompting of the Holy Spirit!

After the meeting, still a little stunned, Ken met for the first time a man called Dick Mills. They arranged to have breakfast together the next day, and in the meantime, Ken busied himself sightseeing with some friends. The morning's warning faded a little in his mind. Perhaps it had only been a coincidence?

Next day, he and Dick Mills met for breakfast; but they had no sooner begun to eat than Dick laid down his knife and fork and began to prophesy. The things he said astonished Ken, private things that Dick had no natural way of knowing, matters Ken had not shared even with me. No one knew them but God and Ken - and now Dick!

One of the many things Dick told Ken was that God did indeed want him to go ahead and write the books he felt compelled to write. Further, Dick decided to encourage Ken in his desire to write. He offered to help by buying some reference books Ken needed. The cost was around $200, a considerable sum in 1974.

Dick did not have the money, but he ordered the books, trusting that God would provide. The next day as he was walking down the street a man stopped him. "Hello Dick", he said, "I would like to pay back the $200 I have owed you for some time." It certainly was a long time, so long that Dick had forgotten the debt! He rejoiced, both for himself and for Ken, at this confirmation of God's leading.

So Ken returned to Australia with a pile of new books, and a clear direction established for his future ministry.

Seventh Fallacy

"GUIDANCE COMES BY DIRECT REVELATION"

> Unto us is born a Son,
> King of quires supernal,
> See on earth his life begun,
> Of lords the Lord eternal.
>
> This did Herod sore affray,
> And grievously bewilder,
> So he gave the word to slay,
> And slew the little childer.
>
> O and A! and A and O!
> Cum cantibus in choro,
> Let our merry organ go,
> Benedicamus Domino![163]

Nowhere does scripture more sadly show the caprice and mystery of human life than in Herod's Slaughter of the Innocents. How black was that night when the cruel king

---

[163] From a 16th century latic carol, translated by G. R. Woodward. The full carol, of course, has several more stanzas. The expression "O and A" is shorthand for "Alpha and Omega", as a more recent translation of the chorus by Percy Dearmer shows -

> Omega and Alpha He!
> Let the organ thunder,
> While choir with peels of glee
> Doth rend the air asunder

"slew the little childer"! How terrible the piteous cries of the bereaved mothers! Matthew's doleful words are altogether heartrending -

> "When Herod saw that the magi had tricked him, he fell into a furious rage and issued an order to kill all the male children in Bethlehem and its neighborhood who were two years old or less. He based this order on the calculations the magi had given him. Then the prediction of the prophet Jeremiah was fulfilled—
>
> *"Listen to the cry coming from Rama,*
> *The bitter mourning and shrieks of lament!*
> *It is Rachel weeping for her children*
> *And refusing to be comforted,*
> *Because they are no more."*[164]

Mark the contrast between those words and our present celebration of Christmas. Merrily (as the carol says) the organ plays, and we Christians sing with peels of joy, "Unto us is born a Son"*! But the Nativity we extol brought no gladness to those anguished parents. The coming of the Christ-child was to them no harbinger of happiness. The "quires supernal" might sing "Peace on earth!" but Rachel has ears only for the wails of her dying infants.*

How some of those parents must have hated the Baby whose birth brought such cruel death to their children! Would you offer them a pine tree clothed in pretty lights for consolation? Could you tell them the brutal slaughter of their little ones was a necessary adjunct to the safe

---

[164] Matthew 2:16-18

arrival of Mary's Child? Or perhaps this would suffice: a pious announcement that God had some deep purpose to fulfill through those tiny dismembered corpses?

Ah! in the face of such loathsome wickedness, in the presence of such fathomless grief, all words, wise and foolish alike, fall empty to the ground. To Rachel, refusing to be comforted, the sweetest syllables are a mockery. Whether the counsel of the intelligent, or the babblings of an imbecile, her ears stay equally deaf. How can mere speech lessen the agony of one who is being broken on the wheel of life's fiercest sorrows?

One thing alone has power to rise above the clamor of such grief; not a word, but an event: Calvary. There, in the vision of the Crucified One, the weeping heart finds, not an explanation, but satisfaction. The mystery of pain remains, for even from his lips burst the awful cry, "My God, my God, why have you abandoned me?"[165] Yet his lament silences our complaint. Just as we are about to shake an angry fist at God, demanding why he allows such horrors to continue, the wounded Savior stands before us. "Have you been treated unfairly, and have you suffered unjustly?" he asks. "My pain was worse. Did you walk death's black valley? My darkness was more awful. Has brutal hatred assaulted you? Behold my wounds!" Injustice, barbarity, violence, cursing, rejection -the torment of all these, and more, the Lord God himself has endured in Christ. We can drink no cup more bitterly than the one he too drank to the last drop.[166]

---

[165] Matthew 27:46.
[166] Luke 22:41-44.

GOD HAS SUFFERED TOO!

Thus the Lord drains all strength out of our protests. Since he cannot yet rid the world of its hurt,[167] he came down among us and made himself its victim. Three days later, his resurrection opened the door into everlasting bliss for all who believe in him. One day we will pass through that door, and then mortality and corruption will be no more, nor tears even remembered.[168]

Meanwhile, during these years of pilgrimage, all of us are vulnerable to injury; none are immune from hurt. Even those whose days are mostly pleasant and free of pain must be chilled by grief's shadow if they but open their eyes. Look, and you will see the infinite despair of children dying of hunger. Listen, and you will hear the cries of battered and broken young people. Bare your heart, and you will feel the relentless pain that wracks the victims of this world's iniquity. Their groans will rise in your own soul, their tears will spring to your own eyes.

We look away from this misery because we must, otherwise laughter would vanish from the world. But in moments of sober reflection, we feel constrained to echo John Bradford, who five hundred years ago saw a group of wretched prisoners plodding to the gallows. As they clanked past him in chains he exclaimed, "There but for the grace of God go I." Is that not true of us all?

Why do I write these things? Not because I do not expect good things from God, for I do. How could I ever tell the

---

[167] Some reasons for this are given in another book of mine. Angels and Demons. One day of course, "All tears will be wiped away" (Revelation 21:1-4), but that blessed hour has not yet come.
[168] 1 Corinthians 15:51-57.

wonder of all that the Father has done for me and my family! Today also, and tomorrow, I look to him for prosperity and health.[169] I live by faith: I expect him to guide me, I trust him to answer my prayers, I ask him to supply bountifully everything I need day by day, I press eagerly toward the magnificent prize that lies ahead in Christ.

Yet there remains a need to disturb the complacent simplicity many Christians cling to in their view of life. They hold tenaciously to the opinion - no matter what happens to their neighbors - that all must go well for them. No sickness can trouble their house, no burglar can steal their goods, no adversity can abridge their happiness. Is not God on their side? How can the Evil One touch them? They conveniently forget that scripture affirms God's alliance within a context of *"tribulation, distress, persecution, famine, nakedness, peril, sword, and slaughter"!*[170] The Father loves you, and cannot withdraw his love, nor allow you to be separated from it. But he is free to express that love either by rescuing you from affliction, or by giving you strength in it. Either way, with Paul, we pronounce ourselves *"more than conquerors*

---

[169] 3 John 2, and scores of similar references.

[170] Romans 8:31, 35-37. Notice how the passage begins and ends with a declaration of God's unfailing love in Christ. Divine love is the framework within which all these troubles occur! God shows his love, not so much by steering us around trouble (although he does do that), as by carrying us unscathed (spiritually) through it. One notable exception to this general principle is found in the healing covenant. God has made special provision to cope with the problem of sickness and disease. I believe firmly that physical healing, as well as spiritual pardon, can be found at the Cross. Yet even here there is warfare to be waged. Just as many spiritual and physical foes hinder us from living fully in the righteousness of Christ, so those same foes often hinder, or even prevent, us from enjoying the full potential of his healing promise. See my book Healing in the Whole Bible, and also the comments below that begin the last chapter of this book.

through Christ."

> "Your joy is your sorrow unmasked.
> And the selfsame well from which your laughter arises was oftentimes filled with your tears.
> And how else can it be?
> The deeper that sorrow carves into your being, the more joy you can contain.
> Is not the cup that holds your wine the very cup that was burned in the potter's oven?
> And is not the lute that soothes your spirit, the very wood that was hollowed with knives?"[171]

A VOICE IN YOUR EAR

A frequent corollary of a simplistic worldview is an expectation of constant guidance from God. We have looked at some aspects of this fallacy in earlier chapters. Here I want to explore the flawed proposition: *"guidance is available through supernatural revelation."*

That assumption is not wholly false. Many references in both Testaments show God guiding his servants by a miracle, either of providence or of revelation: see Isaiah 30:20-21[172]; Luke 2:26-27; Acts 8:26,29; 9:10 ff; 10:19-22; 11:12; 16:7; 20:22; 21:4; 13:4; etc. But let this stand for them all: *"Paul went up to Jerusalem in response to a revelation."*[173]

---

[171] Kahlil Gibran, The Prophet; Alfred A. Knopf, New York, 1968; pg. 29.
[172] Other references from the Old Testament could include God's personal instructions to Abraham, Isaac, Jacob, Joseph, Moses, Samuel, David, Solomon, Hezekiah, Daniel - to name just a few who come quickly to mind.
[173] Galatians 2:1-2.

I am sure every genuine believer has experienced such supernatural guidance at least once, if not often. Certainly Alison and I have. That is not the question. The real problem is this: was Paul *always* so directly guided, and what should our approach be to such supernatural dictates? This is where the fallacy arises: not in the *idea* of supernatural guidance (which is biblical), *but expecting that it must or will always occur.* Why is that wrong?

A MARVELLOUS DIVERSITY

There truly *are* many examples of God miraculously guiding his people, and wonderfully protecting them. But the Lord does not act so obviously nor so frequently that faith is no longer needed. Nor is the same pattern of protection and guidance observable in each believer. It is not even always the same for a single believer. The same Paul who was sometimes guided by a supernatural "word" from God was at other times left in darkness.[174] Thus there are not enough miracles to prevent an unbeliever from dismissing them all as coincidence. Nor are there so many that Christians no longer have to learn how to trust God when he seems to have forsaken them, or worse, when he seems to have lied to them![175]

Suppose *every* Christian were always supernaturally guided and supernaturally protected. Suppose no ill could *ever* befall a believer. Where would faith be? How could we ever learn true confidence in the Father's beneficence? How could praise and worship ever transcend a superficial and juvenile delight in pretty baubles?

---

[174] See for example Philippians 1:19-27, where Paul expressed deep uncertainty, both about the decisions he should make, and what the future would bring him.
[175] Notice the bitter complaint in Jeremiah 15:17-18.

Are we only to thank God when all is well in our affairs? Or can we learn to call him Father even in the melancholy vale of sorrows, trusting that out of the most bewildering twists of fate he is building his own high purpose?[176]

T. H. White, in his vivid retelling of the legends of Camelot, illustrated this same idea. "Wart" (the young Arthur) complained to his tutor, Merlin the wizard, about being favored above his older companion, Kay. Merlin had been giving the Wart many wonderful adventures, while ignoring Kay, and the Wart felt this was unfair. Merlin replied, "It is unfair" - but that is what life is like. Then Merlin told a parable about the prophet Elijah and the Rabbi Jachanan, who slept one night at the home of a poor man. Their host showed them great hospitality, yet in the morning his cow was found dead. It seemed a poor reward for his friendship.

The next evening the two men stayed at the house of a miser, who forced them to sleep in a cowshed and gave them only bread and water. Yet in the morning Elijah "thanked him very much for what he had done, and sent for a mason to repair one of his walls."

The rabbi spoke his perplexity at these incongruous rewards. Elijah explained that in the providence of God the cow's death had saved the life of the poor man's wife, while the rebuilt wall had hidden a chest of gold, which otherwise the miser would have found. So in the end, what seemed unfair proved to be a proper recompense for each man's deeds.[177]

---

[176] Hebrews 13:15. Notice the phrase, "a sacrifice of praise." That is, a heart to praise God when the last thing on earth you feel like doing is rejoicing in the Lord!

[177] The Once and Future King, Book Club Associates, London, 1974; pg. 84,85.

We must learn to trust the ultimate justice of God. There may well be a hidden purpose, a deeper design in the things that happen to us, whether or not we can perceive it. But even if many happenings are mere chance, we are still called to hold fast our confidence in God. One way or another he bends every event toward the fulfillment of his higher purpose.

The same perplexing mystery, and the same demand for unwavering faith, is found in the biblical story of:

THE MURDERED PROPHET

Have you ever pondered the dramatic history of the prophet Uriah?[178] He *"prophesied in the name of the Lord"*, declaring God's true word against the land, the people, the city, and the king. A price was put upon his head, and he fled to Egypt, but the king sent a squad of police after him. They captured him, brought him back to Jerusalem, foully murdered him, and tossed his corpse into an unmarked grave. Yet in the very next verse it says-

> *"Nonetheless, the hand of Ahikam the son of Shapham was with Jeremiah, that the y should not give him into the hand of the people to put him to death."*[179]

One prophet perished, another escaped. Why? Some have said it was because Uriah acted the coward and fled to Egypt; therefore God allowed him to be taken and executed. That is unfair. Joseph and Mary fled to Egypt with Jesus, when Herod threatened the child's life. Was

---
[178] Jeremiah 26:20-22.
[179] Verse 24, KJV

that cowardice, or was it prudence? Anyhow, nothing in scripture shows that Uriah could have saved his life had he remained in Jerusalem. And what about all those prophets and saints across the ages who *did* refuse to flee, or were unable to, yet still suffered violent death?

The real difference between Uriah and Jeremiah was not the fear of one against the faith of the other. Both men possessed faith; they each displayed courage and integrity. Scripture itself shows the real difference between them: Uriah was a poor man, born among farmers, with no influence in high places; Jeremiah was a man of wealth and position. Uriah was a companion of peasants; Jeremiah moved in the upper echelons of society - he claimed a prince as his friend. Although the king imprisoned Jeremiah for a time, he dared not put him to death; the prophet had too many powerful supporters.

Was any specific divine action involved in the fate of either man? Apparently not. One lived, the other died, simply because of their respective social stations. It was unjust and unfair, but life is like that. Scripture records the fact, without approving it. The time has not yet come for God to balance his accounts - except partially and occasionally. The hour of full reckoning still lies before us. On that coming day Uriah, and all who have unjustly suffered at the hands of the wicked, will be fully recompensed.

For now, though, the story of Uriah shows us how God usually lets things go their way, whether for good or evil, without directly interfering with them. I do not mean that he ignored what happened to Uriah. Surely the Father was with his abused servant, filling him with peace, ministering to him in love. Surely the Holy Spirit was there in prison, responding to Uriah's faith, consoling him with hope, giving him courage to die bravely. Yet his colleague Jeremiah escaped peril and continued to prophesy, while the Lord did nothing to prevent Uriah's capture and death.

So Uriah's fate offers no comfort to those who want God to take control over their every step, or to shape every event that happens to them. Such a high level of divine intervention in our daily affairs is not a biblical idea. What then *does* the Bible say? Just this: while the Lord *may* and sometimes *does* act before an event, to shape it and control it, his more normal procedure is to act *after* the event. Think about this verse -

GOVERNED BY GOD

"God works everything together for the good of those who love him."[180]

No matter how you look at Paul's words you see the same thing: most things happen independently of any direct intervention by God. That is, the Lord first lets things occur, then he does with them whatever he pleases. The point is, *the Father doesn't have to control things in advance.* No matter what happens, he is so great, so wise, so powerful, he can bring irresistibly out of any event his wonderful purpose. Was this hurt caused by man, the devil, or natural forces? It makes no difference. For those who love him, the Father turns each episode into a redemptive gift. He makes every incident in your life work for *your* ultimate happiness and *his* highest glory.

---

[180] Romans 8:28.

What would you say about God if he had to control in advance every event, never allowing anything to transpire of its own accord? That would be a sign, not of strength, but of insecurity; it would mark a deity fearful that if he took his hand away, things might get out of control. But of course, that is absurd! Our God timorous and incapable? Preposterous! He shows his vast might and ineffable wisdom by this very fact: he turns the planet loose and all its inhabitants - men and demons alike - and tells them to do whatever they please. He hopes they will freely choose to do his will. But if not, *despite anything they do,* his purpose suffers neither the least delay nor the slightest obstruction. Nothing can thwart the will of the Almighty! That is *real* omnipotence!

Thus God can permit the ordinary principles of cause and effect to have their normal daily outworking without interfering with them. He does not have to keep interrupting life to see that his plans are done. Let those who worship a pygmy deity imagine that he must constantly invade human society, adjusting this, altering that, preventing another, or causing something else. Our glorious God works to his own agenda. No human action can interfere with his ultimate purpose. So let happen what may, the Father's guarantee to his people remains untroubled. *He either works through all things, or makes all things work, for the good of those who love him.* That is the sense of Proverbs like the following -

> *"If you commit everything you do to the Lord, all your plans will be successful ... You may plan your life, but the Lord will have the last word! ... Go ahead and play the game of life, but the winners and losers will be determined*

by God!"[181]

It is difficult to see how the wise man could have written those proverbs, or Paul Romans 8:28, if they had believed that God was acting *before* dawn, shaping each new day according to some pre-ordained purpose. Paul's statement implies that God will control the happenings of tomorrow, not so much in the *morning* as in the *evening*. That is, he leaves me mostly free to live each day as seems best to me. But then, having lived it, whether I did well or poorly, whether the day brought me good or ill, if I give it to the Father, he will take it and transform it into another shimmering step to paradise!

There is nothing here to support an expectation of constant miracles of guidance, nor that God has already mapped out for his children each new day. But there is every encouragement to rejoice in the extraordinary liberty the Father has given us in Christ: the right to forge our own lives, to serve him of our own volition, to come into an astonishing partnership with him in building a destiny of beauty and honor. We can walk with the Father in confident trust. His hand is always there when needed - if not to *alter* the day, then magnificently to *transform* it, so that its outcome will be only good.

Solomon understood this sharp difference between the godly and the ungodly, when he wrote -

> *"A righteous man may fall down seven times, yet he will get up again; but in the end, calamity will utterly destroy the wicked."*[182]

So we should avoid hasty conclusions about what is good

---

[181] Proverbs 16:3,9,33.
[182] Proverbs 24:16.

or bad for us, and about the eventual value of the events of each day. Who knows what God is building out of the bricks of our daily sorrows and joys? Except we know this: God is working in everything for our good! Thus Robert Browning, in the opening lines of his reflective poem, *Rabbi Ben Ezra,* urges a long-term view of life -[183]

> Grow old along with me!
> The best is yet to be,
> The last of life, for which the first was made:
> Our times are in his hands
> Who saith, 'A whole I planned,
> Youth shows but half; trust God: see all, nor be afraid!'

It's too soon to make up your profit and loss account! The story is yet only half told. Wait until all the stones are in place before you judge the worth of the building. The best is yet to be! That beautiful best, that splendid best, for which God is preparing each of his children!

A PRIZE OF WAR

In the 6th century BC the Babylonians crushed Judaic. Towns and villages, farms and orchards, lay in smoldering heaps of scorched ruin. Without mercy, young women were violated and little children driven to harsh labor, until they fell dead from exhaustion.[184] Princes and elders were flayed alive, and their skins pegged on the

---

[183] Had I space to do so, I would quote the entire poem. If you can find a copy and read it, please do. Browning was a "precocious genius", and his poetry, including Rabbi Ben Ezra, is sometimes difficult to grasp. But it is worth the effort to master the poem, which teaches among other things much the same as this book is trying to show: that paradox is an inescapable part of life; that sometimes the best success is found in failure, and the highest joy in pain; and that always the only true fulfillment attainable in life is found in submission to the will of God.

[184] Lamentations 5:11-13.

city wall as a message of terror. Alarm, desolation, misery, rushed unstaunched upon all the people as the invaders enslaved good and evil alike. Indiscriminately the wild soldiers killed young and old; no one was inviolate; the slaughter seemed endless; horror engulfed the nation.

During those hideous months of rapine, Jeremiah's personal servant Baruch learned a humbling lesson. Broken by sorrow and dread, he begged God to save him, his family, his possessions, from the carnage that was devastating Israel. The answer came -

> *"I will overthrow what I have built and pull up what I have sown throughout the land. Why then do you expect some great thing for yourself? Stop asking for it. I intend to bring ruin upon this whole nation; except for this - wherever you go, you may have your life as a prize of war!"*[185]

There was no escape. Baruch had to accept that the savagery of the Babylonians would cost him (as it would every citizen) all his possessions. But at least he would escape with his life - neither slavery nor execution would overtake him. God refused to promise Baruch anything beyond that. Why? What principle rules here?

We are all inescapably part of the society to which we belong. As surely as we share in the benefits of that society when it is prosperous and peaceful, so we must share its sorrows when disaster prowls the land. We cannot altogether dissociate ourselves from our neighbors. We are all to some extent participants both in each other's

---

[185] Jeremiah 45:1-5.

righteousness, and unrighteousness. Thus godly people may bask in the divine commendation of any good the larger community does. But then they must carry also some blame for the evil done by that same community.

Therefore, if God has decreed *"disaster upon all the people"* (as he did to Israel in the time of Baruch), then it is futile for the godly *"to seek some great thing for themselves"*. They will do well enough if they escape with their lives![186]

But this principle is true every day, not just in times of national upheaval. Usually, if it would altogether distance us from our neighbors, we cannot *"seek some great thing"* for ourselves. The threats and perils before which the larger community is vulnerable also approach us.

> *"No man is an island, entire of itself; every man is a piece of the continent, a part of the main; if a clod be washed away by the sea, Europe is the less, as well as if a promontory were, as well as if a manor of thy friends or of thine own were; any man's death diminishes me, because I am involved in mankind; and therefore never send to know for whom the bell tolls; it tolls for thee."*[187]

Sometimes, for a special purpose, the Lord does step in and miraculously rescue one of his servants, but not often. Both Peter and Paul, for example, were supernaturally

---

[186] The same principle was at work when God told Lot and his family to flee from Sodom empty-handed. He forbade them even to look back at the Continued from page 129...burning city (Genesis 19:15-26). Likewise, Jesus warned the Christians that when the time came for Jerusalem to be destroyed, they should abandon everything and flee (Matthew 24:15-19), which history tells us they did.

[187] John Donne (1571?-1631), English poet and divine;

released from prison. But only once each. Later, they were imprisoned again, and finally executed. This time they found no way to escape - although we may suppose they prayed for one, and probably expected, or at least hoped for, another miraculous rescue. But the Lord chose not to intervene.

Or consider the church. When the Roman empire began to crumble under the onslaughts of the barbarians, Christians could not escape the rape and ruin that fell upon the land. The chains of slavery were fastened upon thousands of Christians, who were forced to toil in misery alongside their pagan neighbors. Pillage and sword destroyed Christian homes, just as they did those of the ungodly. Christian maidens were ravished, Christian families torn apart, Christian children sold into brothels, Christian churches smashed to rubble. For every story of miraculous deliverance told by one delighted Christian, there were a hundred others of heart-tearing dolor. If the hand of God was stretched out to rescue one, just as surely it was withheld from another.

Nothing has changed. We remain exposed as they were to the perils of life in a fallen society.

WHERE IS YOUR TREASURE?

Jesus was aware of human vulnerability, which is why he gave the warning -

> *"Don't store your treasures on earth, where moth and rust can destroy them, and where they can be stolen by thieves. Deposit your riches in heaven, where moth and rust cannot harm them, and robbers cannot break in and*

steal them"[188]

Does Christ promise that you can protect your earthly wealth and happiness if only you have enough faith? Does he tell you how to build a spiritual barrier around your home that no burglar can penetrate? No, he knew nothing of such nonsense. He realized that the goods and prosperity of the righteous are as likely as those of the unrighteous to be destroyed by corruption and violence. Such sorrows are endemic in this sin-troubled world. We possess no promise of absolute protection; scripture offers no secret *"great thing"* to God's servants. You will ordinarily look in vain for some impenetrable defense to stand behind. Unless God chooses for his own ends to drive off the thief, the same loss may fall upon you as upon your neighbor.

Does God *never* drive away the thief? Of course he does! How often? Who can tell! Sometimes his protection is obvious. More often it is unobtrusive. Perhaps mostly, we Christians enjoy peace, safety, and prosperity for more ordinary reasons -

<u>first</u>: because we live in a well-ordered society, which has been heavily influenced by the gospel;

<u>second</u>: because those who join the church tend to move into a different position in society, where they are more likely to flourish;

<u>third</u>: because the Holy Spirit is constantly at work in our lives, changing our attitudes, making us a people of faith and diligence who are likely to prosper;

---

[188] Mathew 6:19-20

fourth: because the Father most certainly is active every day, answering prayer, meeting needs, giving strength, and the like.[189]

I am sure the Father more often than not does concern himself with our affairs, and helps us in countless ways, even with a miracle if necessary. I am saying only that no guarantee is visible either in life or scripture that his intervention will always take the shape we think it should. God cannot be pinned down to such a predictable response.[190] Thus, one young woman, threatened by a foul rapist, cries out, *"Jesus, save me!"* -and her attacker flees, cringing from some nameless terror.

Some girls have told how angels came to fight for them, and there was nothing left for them to do except to rejoice in the Lord's deliverance.

But other women have called upon the sacred name in vain, and found no one to prevent the fulfillment of their assailant's vile intent. What went wrong? Did one girl speak in faith, but the other in unbelief? What a wretched judgment that would be! Narrow-minded, insulting, insensitive - there are hardly enough epithets to describe self-righteous critics who offer such flawed verdicts.

I cannot say why the name of Jesus causes one rapist to run away, while another is undeterred. I know only that church history and personal observation alike confirm the lack of any constant pattern. God may intervene or he may not - there seems no way to predict either the one or the other. We are entitled to hold a general confidence in

---

[189] Compare the Lord's Prayer, Matthew 6:9-13, which presupposes the Father's daily involvement in our lives.
[190] Isaiah 55:8-9.

the Father's guidance and care, which is why most Christians do enjoy a long life of health and happiness. But that confidence must fall short of certainty, for we do not know what each new day will bring.[191] You yourself know good people, godly people, as I do, who have been overwhelmed by unexpected tragedy.[192] No reason can be given for their sorrow, except that God chose not to prevent it.

Perhaps the hardest task I ever had was to counsel a young Christian wife who, twice within the same week, had been raped by an intruder while her husband was at work. This foul violation of their sanctity had shattered both of them. Their formerly happy home became a place of haunted shame, their dreams a nightmare. Where was God? Why had he not protected her? Didn't he care? How could he watch her being brutalized and do nothing to prevent it? Could they ever trust him again?

The young husband left his job (which had involved much night work), and they moved to the other side of the country. They wanted to get as far away as possible from the place of their humiliation. That is when I met them - their marriage collapsing; their minds torn by endless questions and accusations; both blaming each other; both blaming themselves. Perhaps the fault was God's? Or was

---

[191] James 4:13-17. You will find a comment on this passage just below

[192] For some biblical examples, note the sad end of the godly King Josiah (2 Kings 23:28-29); and the destruction of the fleet of the righteous Jehoshaphat (1 Kings 22:47). With the benefit of hindsight, the Chronicler found reason to attribute some of the fault for their mishaps to the two kings (2 Chronicles 20:35-37; 35:20-24). But the author of Kings offered no blame. At the time, the monarchs thought their actions were in the best interests of the people. Jeremiah's reaction was more sympathetic. When Josiah was killed, "he composed a lament ... and to this day the minstrels, both men and women, commemorate Josiah in their lamentations" (2 Chronicles 35:25, REB).

it the devils? They had no answers; their lives were falling apart.

It was many weeks before they confided in me. But when they did, their first question was, *"why?"* What could I say? I don't know why, except that life is sometimes saturated with pain, even for the children of God. You will not find a solution by seeking *"some great thing"* that isolates you from your community. Rather, even in the darkest valley of the shadow of death, look for the comforting rod and staff of the Good Shepherd. He too has trodden the vale of hatred, brutality, and humiliation. We must find satisfaction and victory, as he did, by faith's trustful cry: *"Father, into your hands I commit my spirit!"*[193]

With words like those I encouraged my young friends, and they found faith again, and today, many years later, they are still actively serving the Lord. Like Job, their happiness and prosperity have been restored, and the Lord has blessed them with many riches, both material and spiritual.

But does every story have such a happy ending? Think about this -

TIME AND CHANCE HAPPENS TO ALL

One pastor, popular, personable, manipulative, self-promoting, receives a gift of $500,000, which he promptly uses to buy a magnificent house; while another man, humble, diligent, gentle, sacrificial, struggles with poverty all his life. Or, a missionary starves out on the field, while a crass compromiser lives in opulent luxury -

---

[193] Luke 23:46.

and so on. I could cite a hundred such examples, and you could cite a hundred more. From our perspective, life is full of such disparities. Do these variances arise from an express purpose of God, or do they simply reflect a topsy turvy world, in which the highest rewards often go to the wrong people?

There is a situation even more difficult to bear: people who are equal in devotion and faithfulness to the Lord, and equal in talent, yet a wide gap exists between their achievements and also their rewards. One goes from triumph to triumph; the other toils for a meager harvest. How bitter life can become when constant disappointment has blighted eager hope, when frustration is made more painful by the success of people no more, and perhaps even less, deserving of it.[194]

It comes to this: we may have a general expectation of good things in life, and of divine protection;[195] but no one can absolutely say, *"I will always prosper; I will never lose my job, or never have an auto crash; no thief will ever enter my home; no hurt or loss will ever touch me."* You may perhaps be so fortunate. But you cannot be sure of it. Shipwreck swamped even Paul three times! James also, warns us about the uncertainty of each new day -

> *"Listen to me. why do you say, 'Today or tomorrow I will go to this city, or to that one, stay for a year, set up a business there, and make a good profit'? How can you make such a boast when you don't even know what tomorrow will bring? ... Rather, you ought to*

---

[194] I am talking, of course, about things as we see them. God plainly has a different viewpoint. Yet we can judge only what we see; and from where we look, life is full of anomalies and disparities.

[195] Compare 3 Jn 2; Jn15:16; 16:24; and many other references.

say, 'If the Lord pleases, I will keep on living, and do this, or that.' So stop strutting around and flaunting your confidence. There is nothing but sin in that kind of talk."[196]

Many other scriptures have the same import. They warn the righteous to be ready for affliction.[197] They counsel the wise man to gather his harvest in the summer, to thatch his roof before the rain starts[198] These passages, whether they deal with general providence or specific persecution, accept the premise that *"man is born to trouble as surely as sparks fly upward".*[199]

Does this mean you should get out of bed each morning with a gloomy apprehension of misfortune? Of course not. Christian life should be a confident expectation of good things from the hand of a benevolent Father. That is how Jesus himself taught us to pray in the Lord's Prayer; and that is what many biblical promises encourage us to believe. Nonetheless, an element of uncertainty remains. Solomon's observation remains undeniable -

> *"After pondering these things I finally concluded that God truly holds in his hand the lives of those who are wise and righteous; yet not one of them knows whether tomorrow will bring love or hate ... I have also observed this happening under the sun: a swift man loses the race, and a mighty man falls in battle. I have seen hunger gripping a wise man, a brilliant man deprived of wealth, and those who are skilful stripped of honor. Time*

---
[196] 4:13-16.
[197] Psalm 34:19; John 16:33; Acts 14:22; plus many others.
[198] Proverbs 6:6-8; 10:4-5; 30:25; 27:12.
[199] Job 5:7.

and chance happen to everyone, nor does anyone know when his hour will come."[200]

What a strange yet true conclusion Solomon reached! He decided to accept two things that seem to contradict each other:

- on one side, "God truly holds in his own hand the lives of the righteous;"
- on the other, "Not one of them knows whether tomorrow will bring love or hate!"

Is there a quarrel between those ideas? No, for they express the mystery of life. Like you, I believe with all my heart that my days are in God's hand, and I always expect (and ask for) good things from him. Yet I cannot know what each hour will bring. Perhaps laughter, perhaps tears; perhaps triumph, perhaps tragedy. But I am speaking only of life's surface, which may today be placid and tomorrow stormy; but far below, in the fathomless depths of God's love, the sea is always serene. So in the end, I can neither be truly defeated nor despoiled, for my real hope is anchored in Christ, where no earthly vicissitude can ever reach!"[201]

---

[200] Ecclesiastes 9:1,11-12. Quoted also in chapter three, above.
[201] Hebrews 6:18-20.

Discovery

Alison's Story

AN ADVENTURE FOR GOD!
(Sydney & the USA, 1978-1982)

Our Bible Correspondence Course was born in 1974. We began with nothing, no money, no equipment, but with a group of wonderful people, our friends in Launceston, who were willing to stand with us, work hard, and sacrifice to make our vision possible. As each new book was written our student body grew, until now the books have gone into 25 different countries. Several of them have been translated into other languages, and thousands of people have been taught and enriched by them.

The visions of the light and the tree are still being fulfilled! However, while the program was born in Launceston, four years later the Lord showed us that the time had come to move into a larger sphere. The word from God came while Ken was attending a conference in Singapore. He felt the Lord was telling him to move to Sydney, and to join Vision Ministries,[202] under the direction of Alan Langstaff.

Meanwhile, at home during my quiet time, God had directed me to a verse in Genesis (28:15). Behold. I am with thee and will keep thee in all places whither thou goest <u>and will bring thee attain into this land</u>. For I will not leave thee until I have done that which I have spoken

---

[202] This organization was founded by Alan and Dorothy Langstaff, and during the late '70s it was the most significant interdenominational charismatic ministry in Australia. VM was especially renowned for its great conferences that were attended by as many as 15, 000 people, from all parts of the church in Australia.

of. I underlined this verse, not realizing then its significance, but knowing the Lord had a message in it just for me.

When Ken arrived home from Singapore, the Lord quickened the verse to me again and I went to look it up. I had no doubt the Father was leading us, and the time had come to move. So we shifted house to Sydney and we both joined the staff of Vision Ministries. Ken also was appointed president of Vision Bible College. The correspondence course continued to expand steadily.

WE MOVE TO AMERICA

Less than two years after we arrived in Sydney, Alan and Dorothy Langstaff, with their children, moved to Minneapolis in the USA. Their goal was to expand Vision Ministries internationally. They invited us to join with them, saying that our correspondence course was needed there. Several American friends had also urged us to do this, because of the lack of a similar program in their country.

"Come on Mum, let's go. It'll be fun," clamored the children. My husband looked at me across their heads.

"It's your decision, Honey. I think we should go, but I'll wait until you feel it's right."

When any momentous decision had to be made concerning our family, Ken would just wait patiently, either until I agreed with him, or we both decided to drop the idea. He knew that if the decision he had made was God's leading, then God would also show me.

My spirit was in turmoil. How could I feel good about

leaving my country, my oldest son, my parents, and the rest of my family, to go to the USA, perhaps for many years, perhaps forever!

Our daughter Sharon was 20 years of age; what if she decided to marry in the USA? What of our sons, Eric and Baden, their education, their future? For days and nights I walked up and down my living room, pleading with the Lord to show me his will.

One morning I left my bed early, agitated, and unable to sleep. I was kneeling in the living room of our home in Lillee Pillee, exhausted from grappling with the thoughts that continually tumbled through my mind. In the still quietness of the early morning God spoke to my heart. His voice was unmistakable, and so reasonable, so reassuring.

"You are trying to look too far ahead. Don't look ahead twenty years but just two years. I promise you that after two years you will either be coming home, or you will want to stay."

Enormous relief filled my heart! All my burden and anxiety vanished. Two years would be fun, an adventure to be enjoyed, not an imposition to be endured. I woke Ken and told him what had happened, and he rejoiced with me at this unusual answer to my prayer.

Over the next few weeks we said a sad farewell to our son, Dale, who was still pursuing his Ph.D. at Monash University, and to our family and friends in Australia.

We didn't take much with us - Ken's books, some blankets, our clothing, and some silverware. Almost everything else we gave away.

Five days after our arrival in the USA, Eric became violently ill. We had noticed that he was not his usual brisk and happy self, but had thought this was a natural reaction to leaving his friends. Throughout the night his condition deteriorated until, in the early morning, we had no alternative but to contact a doctor. The verdict was immediate. Eric was not even permitted to return for his toothbrush. Instead he was rushed into emergency for an operation to remove his appendix!

Piling poverty on misery we discovered that, for the first time in Ken's frequent trips overseas, no traveler's insurance had been taken out for us. This meant that only the amount covered by our Australian medical insurance was at our disposal. The difference was $2,100!

Right about now several people might question our trip to the USA, but I knew God had spoken to me, so we were not crushed. In fact this incident opened up the hearts of the American people to us in an exceptional way. We were given the loan of a car, and on our finding a suitable house, they showed their generosity by giving us the furniture we needed to set up our home. From several different people the money was given to us to pay Eric's medical bill. The Lord had turned a potential tragedy into a triumph!

PERILS IN A STRANGE LAND

Just two months after our arrival in the USA, and shortly after settling into our new home, Sharon and I drove Ken to the airport. He had to fly to Singapore to teach for two weeks at a Bible School.

By this time we had bought a second-hand Oldsmobile, and Sharon had mastered driving on the right hand side

Discovery

of the road. She felt confident that she could find her way home after saying our goodbyes to Ken at the terminal. I did not feel competent as yet to drive, so I gladly yielded her the wheel. (In fact, two years passed before I grew brave enough for the freeways. Due to some strange proclivity, as a left-hander I continually mistake my right hand for my left!)

So Sharon took over, and soon she and I were on our way home. Only a mile down the road the dashboard light warned us the engine was running hot. We pulled in to the nearest service station. In our innocence we did not realize that this was just a gas station without a competent mechanic. We asked for help and the attendant lifted the bonnet and began to unscrew the radiator. Even I knew that was not wise! The cap shot into the air, and because of a slight tilt in my direction the contents hit me in the face. Hot water mixed with anti-freeze is not the nicest combination to strike face and hair! Soaking, my eyes filled with the solution, I staggered to the ladies room and washed myself. Worse was to come!

The gas attendant filled up the car radiator again and insisted that we would have no more trouble. We drove off obediently, but barely a mile down the road the red light blinked again, and we knew that we would have to get help.

Panic seized me as we drove off the freeway. This was unfamiliar territory. The street seemed poor and unkempt. My memory began to stir with accounts of robberies and murders. The people all around us seemed unfriendly. We parked the car and I made Sharon lock herself in while I attempted to find someone to rescue us. I walked nervously down the street -remember I am an

Australian, and I had read some lurid tales about America! I was convinced that everyone carried a gun, and would need little excuse to use it!

Finally I reached a service station and asked to use the telephone. Imagine my horror when I opened the phone book and found not one of the people I knew listed. We lived in the Minneapolis part of the Twin Cities and we had driven into St. Paul. The people I knew were all in Minneapolis, and the service station had no telephone book for that city. Wet and cold from my dowsing, miserable and afraid, I cried out to God. Immediately he reminded me that only the Sunday before we had met a friendly couple from Texas, and they had given me their phone number.

"If we can be of any help, then let us know."

Those were the words that rang in my ears. Of course, they lived in St. Paul! Quickly I pulled out my pocket diary and found the phone number, my voice a little wobbly by this time.

Later, at home, showered and warm, I thanked God for his thoughtful provision. Of course I thanked my Texan friends as well. They were truly used by God to rescue this timid Australian from her difficulty.

Eighth Fallacy

"LOOK FOR THE APPROVAL OF TWO OR THREE COUNSELLORS"

Who can plumb the mystery of God's omnipotence? We have seen how the Lord can turn the whole world loose, to do whatever it pleases, yet nothing on earth even slightly threatens his announced purpose! Always he is bringing order out of chaos!

The manner in which the Lord writes his ultimate design upon each Christian's life can be seen by looking around you. Everywhere you turn in nature you will see the same rule at work: *random events becoming a pattern.* A group of frenzied atoms fuses into a liquid molecule; a cluster of haphazard molecules combines into a drop of water; countless drops of water, falling irregularly, become a pond - and so on.

Many studies have shown that while a single event may be unpredictable, a mass of events always resolves into a fixed shape. Insurance companies use this law. No one can say what will happen to one 55-year old man, whether he will live ten years or twenty. But if you take a million men in their middle fifties, statisticians can predict with great accuracy how many of them will reach their seventieth year.

I saw an experiment on television once, in which a technician dropped some colored balls down a chute. When he used only a few balls, no pattern was observable; the balls seemed to fall randomly. The same was true when he increased the number of balls a few score. But when hundreds of them fell into the tray below, a clear pattern began to emerge. The behavior of a single ball was unpredictable; the behavior of a mass of them followed a fixed law. Yet it was possible, of course, for the operator to choose one ball, exert influence upon it, and so decide where and when that ball should fall. For example, if he wanted a red ball to lodge in a certain position and stay there, he could guide its motion sufficiently to get that result.

This law seems to be true at both the atomic and cosmic levels, and for almost everything between, including human beings. The behavior of a million atoms follows an invariable design; but the fate of one atom cannot be known, unless something gains control over it. The direction of one vehicle on the freeway cannot be told; but traffic engineers accurately predict the motion of thousands of them. One asteroid may be hewed fantastically; but astronomers will tell you exactly what shape a billion of them merged will take. Out of chaos comes order. Always the divine principle is this: into a world without form, and void, the Lord God speaks an organizing decree.[203]

---

[203] Genesis 1:1-3. The same idea can be argued from a different perspective, using the latest concepts of "chaos theory", particular in conjunction with the extraordinary patterns created by Professor Mandelbrot in the mathematical designs known as the "Mandelbrot Set". There the idea is rather that within each single, or simple, item there lies a limitless complexity. It can perhaps be described as an unbroken circle of chaos to unity to chaos. Thus an almost boundless diversity and flexibility is maintained within a unifying principle.

Discovery

Since these things represent the way the Father has chosen to structure the universe, why suppose that a different principle rules in the church? While single events in our lives may seem random, and unpredictable, their accumulation builds slowly and irrevocably into God's ordained design. The behavior of particular Christians may lack any visible conformity to a pattern; but the church, a composite of millions of believing units, irresistibly takes the shape God has decreed.

Because of this law, God can give great freedom of choice to each Christian. What each person does neither hinders nor prevents the destiny of the church. Likewise, under normal conditions, how you and I behave each day will not undo the final goal God has set for us. I say "under normal conditions" because we do possess a volition that atoms, colored balls, and stars lack. Remember that all things conform to the pattern unless some outside force influences them. In our case, that "outside force" may be either our own action, or God's.

I see it this way. If I am in fellowship with the Father, and doing the best I can to walk in his ways, then I may trust him to bring out of my life a result that pleases him. He can do this ordinarily without directly influencing my choices or actions. On the other hand, like the operator above with his red ball, if God does want me in a certain place at a certain time, he can easily get me there. I am yielded enough to his purpose for him easily to take me wherever he wants to, whether or not I am conscious of him doing it.

A key factor in those thoughts is the idea of personal volition. How do we reconcile our free will with divine sovereignty? Certainly not by abandoning our right of choice and viewing ourselves as puppets! If you want to grow up, and please God, and allow him to work his will through your life, then you will need to make more, not fewer, decisions by yourself! But of course, you will need to make them wisely, not stupidly. How to do that is the question.

Some contend that there is safety in numbers. If two or three counselors agree that a particular path is the will of God, then you may safely proceed. Is that a trustworthy rule?

GOOD AND BAD ADVICE

Surely this is good sense: before you make any important decisions, seek the advice of other people: *"In many counselors there is safety"*[204]

But when you do ask for counsel, make sure you go to the right people; that is, turn to those who have earned the right to express an opinion. I have often noticed two groups of silly questioners:

- those who ask advice from people who say only what the enquirer wants to hear; and
- those who ask advice from people who are not qualified to give it.

Search rather for wise, mature, experienced, stable, and honest counselors. As the sage rabbi expressed it -

> *"Who will learn? He who loves to listen. Who will gain wisdom? He who opens his ear. When you attend the assembly of elders, look*

---

[204] See Proverbs 11:14; 15:22; 24:6; especially in the NEB.

> *out for a wise man. If you find one, don't let go of him! ... Visit his home at daybreak! Wear a pathway across his doorstep! Never forsake the man who possesses mature insight!"*[205]

I came across that piece of wisdom when I was still a teen-ager, over forty years ago. It gripped me, and I promised myself and God to do just what Sirach advised: find people who knew more than I did, and cling to them until I had tapped their knowledge. I have never abandoned that quest. The years have now drawn me beyond many of my earlier counselors; but my way is still constantly crossed by people wiser than I. My feet still wear a path across the doorstep of such people! I ask, and learn and, I hope, grow yet wiser myself.

Don't be deceived by mere age, nor by those who boast of their wisdom. An ancient English proverb warns, *"There is no fool like an old fool"* - especially an old fool who thinks he knows it all! You will have found a true pundit, not when you meet one who proclaims the vastness of his knowledge, but one who confesses with Lao Tzu, *"The further I go, the less I know."*[206] The truly learned understand how little they have learned!

> *"(Hold fast to) modesty. Never think that you already know it all. However highly you are appraised, always have the courage to say to yourself - I am ignorant!"*[207]

Perhaps because it does take courage to admit error or

---
[205] Sirach 6:32-37.
[206] Lao Tzu was a Chinese philosopher who flourished six hundred years before Christ.
[207] The great scientist Ivan Petrovich Pavlov, in a 1936 document (the year of his death), Bequest to the Academic <u>Youth of Soviet Russia</u>.

ignorance, there are so many who lack wisdom. No one can become enlightened who does not begin by humbly confessing darkness. The rays of dawn shine only across the night sky.

HAVING THE COURAGE OF YOUR CONVICTIONS

A sensibly cautious person needs strong reasons to act against the advice of dependable counselors. Yet those reasons do sometimes appear. Even the cleverest advisers may fail you. You will then find yourself obliged to trust the instruction of your own heart. Omar Khayyam, that remarkable Persian mathematician, philosopher, and poet, told how the wisdom of the wise had often disappointed him -

> Myself when young did eagerly frequent
> Doctor and sage, and heard great argument
> About it and about: but evermore
> Came out by that same door as in I went.
>
> With them the seed of Wisdom did I sow,
> And with my own hand wrought to make it grow:
>
> And this was all the Harvest that I reap'd -
> "I came like Water, and like Wind I go." [208]

Khayyam was an unrepentant cynic, arrogant in his weary rejection of the struggle to grasp wisdom. But a germ of reason lies in his words. In the end there may be no truth greater than what you find within yourself.

Sirach caught the same idea, although he expressed it

---

[208] The Rubaiyat of Omar Khayyam, tr. by Edward Fitzgerald; stanzas 30 & 31.

more positively and pragmatically

> "Have you ever met a counselor who did not say his advice is best? Yet some of them speak only in their own interest, seeking their own advantage. So be wary of the man who offers advice. Find out first if he expects to gain something from his counsel. He may be so bent by a hope of personal profit that any path he guides you toward will be crooked, even if he tells you it will be straight.
>
> "The biased counselor will not follow-through on his counsel; rather, he will step back, then wait to see what happens to you. Be warned therefore -
>
>> "Never trust someone who looks at you slyly;
>> Never confide in a person who envies you;
>> Never ask advice from a woman about her rival;
>> Never consult any of these -
>>> a coward about war,
>>> a shop-keeper about a bargain,
>>> a buyer about your selling price,
>>> a miser about generosity,
>>> a pitiless man about kindness,
>>> an indolent person about toil,
>>> a temporary employee about finishing a job,
>>> a lazy worker about a demanding task.
>
> "Never turn to any of them for advice. Rely rather on a person who fears God, who is obedient to the law of the Lord, who shares your goals and cares about your happiness, who will be there to support you if you fall.

> *"But don't forget to trust your own judgment. No one knows you better than you know yourself!* Who will ever care for you more diligently? Seven watchmen peering from a high tower may sometimes fail to see danger that you can discover by yourself in a moment!
>
> "Above all, pray to the Most High. Trust him to keep you from straying off the pathway of truth."[209]

Here then is the rule: get the best counsel you can from the most capable people you can find; but have the courage also to follow your deepest personal convictions. And never stop asking God to guide your steps. Trustful dependence upon the Father, matched with bold assertion of your right to build your own life, coupled with a humble quest for counsel from good people, should hold you to the right way.

THREE DEFENCES

Balance is everything, both in doctrine and in life. *"Let your sweet reasonableness,"*[210] said Paul, *"be obvious to everybody."* Does someone say that direct, supernatural guidance is always readily available? He goes beyond scripture. Does another say that any kind of immediate direction by God is a myth? He falls short of scripture.

Somewhere there is a fair median, which some may want to press closer to the miraculous than I do, while others

---

[209] Sirach 37:7-15, emphasis mine.
[210] Philippians 4:5. The Greek word is "epieikes", which can be translated many ways, among them (in adjectival form), "gracious, forbearing," hence by extension "reasonable, fair-minded, tolerant."

may prefer to pull further back. Indeed, I wobble myself between one and the other - on this occasion expecting and recognizing the hand of the Father; on another sensing that I must find a solution by myself. The experience of most devout people is probably similar. How can you develop Paul's gracious poise? Where can you find his wise symmetry? Certainly not by leaping to an extreme opinion, nor by fastening upon a single method.

Jeremiah, in one of his diatribes against his enemies, gives an interesting, and unintended, example of this balance. He indirectly reveals the three sources from which sober and godly Israelites expected to find reliable guidance:[211]

- the wise man with his "counsel"
- the priest with the "law"
- the prophet with the "word"

Sensible people still seek a combination of those three things, especially when a decision of importance must be made. That is, they look for a blend of *sound advice*, *scriptural support*, and *prophetic revelation*. When those three agree together, you may usually assume that you are on the right course.[212]

PERSONAL VOLITION

This much is certain: you will surely be misled if you

---

[211] Jeremiah 18:18. See also Ezekiel 7:26, where a similar list is given, showing the three sources of guidance as: prophetic vision; priestly direction; mature counsel.

[212] However, not always. That was the fault of the Jews. Prophet, priest, and counselor were all agreed that Jeremiah was wrong in his threats of coming ruin. The leaders accepted the majority opinion, and persecuted Jeremiah. Sometimes a man or woman has to stand alone, loyal only to the voice of his or her own conscience. More about that later.

settle upon a policy of always demanding infallible guidance, and always by a miracle. Scripture does not permit such an abrogation of your personal responsibility. For better or for worse, God has given us both the right and duty of making our own decisions! Sometimes people seek personal revelation because they feel that their mind and their spirit are at war with each other.

They suppose that instruction that comes to them via their spirit must be superior to ideas conceived in their mind.

Hearken back to Jeremiah's mention of *counsel, law,* and *prophecy* as a source of complete guidance. Let me change the analogy to that of *body, soul,* and *spirit*; that is, the physical, the rational, and the supernatural should come together to form a complete picture of what God wants you to do. Banish the idea that somehow your mind is an enemy of your spirit. Each part of your being should work in harmony together to discover and do the will of God.

The church Fathers understood this better than many Christians do today. In their struggles against the superstitions of the heathen, the soothsaying and wizardry that was all around them, the Fathers strongly emphasized the rational nature of man. *"Here is the chief glory,"* they forcefully argued, *"that belongs to all whom Christ has redeemed: we can discard pagan and childish delusions, and behave reasonably, in response to the word of God."* One of the greatest of the Fathers, Clement of Alexandria, put it this way

> *"Everything that is contrary to right reason is sin ... Christian conduct is the operation of the rational in accordance with correct judgment and aspiration after the truth,*

which attains its destined end through the body, the soul's consort and ally. Virtue is a will in conformity to God and Christ in life, rightly adjusted to life everlasting. For the life of Christians, in which we are now trained, is a system of reasonable actions - that is of those things taught by the Word - an unfailing energy which we have called faith."[213]

Note Clement's view that Christ has now integrated the believer into a harmonious union of body, soul, and spirit, which are no longer at war with each other. He sees the various parts of our nature combining to lead us firmly on in the will of God. In a sense this undivided harmony belongs now, in Christ, to every believer; but in another sense we must each dedicate ourselves to work it out in daily life. Avoid exalting mind above spirit, or spirit above mind; rather, strive to unite spirit, mind, and body in the service of Christ. The more you can draw with equal maturity upon the physical, the rational, and the supernatural to learn his purpose, the closer you will come to a perfect walk before God.

RESIST UNDUE PRESSURE

If heaven suddenly seems in a hurry, you are probably not hearing God, but another voice. If you find yourself under pressure, it is probably *not* the Holy Spirit prompting you. Why should the Lord have to act hastily, when all eternity is at his disposal? Surprise never startles the Lord of glory; events do not abruptly overtake the Almighty and

---

[213] Clement of Alexandria, The Instructor, Bk 1, ch 13; "Ante-Nicene Fathers," vol 2, pg 235(b); Eerdmans Publishing Company, 1978 reprint.

find him unprepared! You can therefore afford to sit back, relax, and take time to think things through carefully. The Holy Spirit will not get angry if you *test* whatever revelation may have come to you -

> *"You should not stifle the Holy Spirit, nor despise prophetic revelations; nevertheless, don't just accept things without question. Examine everything carefully; test everything, so that you keep only what is good, and discard what is false."*[214]

You are far more likely to offend the Lord by hasty action than by pausing for sober reflection. So investigate critically every prompting, whim, dream, or revelation that comes your way. Accept these things as the voice of God only if they conform to other criteria - such as scripture, good counsel, common sense, previous instructions you have received from the Lord, and the like.

Admittedly, it takes time to learn how to distinguish the true from the false; but some Christians take much longer to reach this goal than is necessary. The writer of Hebrews lamented the sluggish understanding of his flock. They exasperated him enough to deserve the insult "blockheads"[215], because they refused to grow up in Christ. He yearned for the day when *"by long experience they would have learned how to distinguish right from wrong"*[216] -people mature enough to be trusted with their own decision making.

---

[214] 1 Thessalonians 5:19-22.
[215] The literal meaning of Hebrews 5:11. Another possible choice: "numskulls". The Greek word is a strong colloquial expression.
[216] Verses 12-14.

There is however an irony here. Getting older doesn't necessarily make getting guidance any easier. Indeed, as the years pass by, one tends toward ever more caution! Mistakes made in the past build an increasing reluctance to accept uncritically everything that looks like a divine revelation! Grey hairs remind you that time is running out, and you cannot afford to make any more errors in judgment! You also remember the harm done by previous hasty actions. You become sensitive to the loss a wrong decision can cause other people, which makes you careful, very careful, about jumping to ill-founded conclusions! At least, that is how it ought to be. Sadly, some people die more ignorant than they were born, locked into stubborn folly, obdurate in their refusal to learn. Happily, you are not among them, otherwise you would not be reading these words!

THE PEACE OF GOD

"The peace of God," says Paul[217], can occupy in your heart the position of a referee or "umpire" (that is the meaning of the Greek word). This "peace" is an important guide, although it is not infallible. You should certainly not depend upon it if it stands alone. As I have already suggested, personal feelings are unreliable, and should be viewed with suspicion, or at least acted on with caution. Paul held the same opinion, so he added two qualifications to the rule of the peace of God:

- this peace should function within your "calling in the one body"; *and*
- this peace should be associated with "the word of Christ dwelling in you richly".

---

[217] Colossians 3:15.

If people are out of fellowship with the church, if they are living contrary to scripture, then any "peace" they feel is delusory. It is not God's peace. When Paul suggests allowing "the peace of God" to referee your decisions, he assumes that you belong to a local church, and that you are well-instructed in, and obedient to, the word of God. Whatever lies outside those criteria creates, not God's peace, but a false security whose end is destruction -

> *"There is a way that seems right to a man, but at its end lies death."*[218]

A CLOUD OR A GUIDE?

Here is something you may never have noticed. Look at Numbers 9:15-23, where three things are outstanding:

first: for forty years God kept control over Israel's movements through the pillars of cloud and fire. Similarly, we too must place our lives under the ultimate, the final, and the absolute control of God. Could any true Christian want less or ask less than this?

second: there was a seeming arbitrariness, unpredictability about the movements of the cloud; the people were unable either to predict or control its apparently erratic actions. Similarly, supernatural guidance sometimes comes to us often, but other times infrequently. During those periods of long silence we can no more compel the Lord to speak than Israel could compel the cloud to move.

third: when the cloud was stationary, and no command was coming from heaven, the people were free to pursue

---

[218] Proverbs 14:12; 16:25.

their private lives and goals. God imposed no hindrance upon them, except they were forbidden to remove themselves from under the cloud. Similarly, unless the Lord has placed in front of us a clear command to "move", we are free to make many choices and decisions on our own. Nonetheless, we should never choose contrary to the larger purpose the Lord has set for our lives.

But having said all that, at once there occurs an arresting change. Look at the very next chapter of Numbers (10:29-34), where, instead of the people following the cloud, suddenly *it is the cloud following the people!*[219] Further, Moses wanted Hobab to travel with them, to be the *"eyes"* of Israel - that is, to act as their guide through the wilderness. Because he was familiar with the country, Hobab knew where to find water, and the like.

What a dramatic turnabout! Suddenly, careful planning and preparation replace ghostly guidance! The fiery cloud is no longer trusted alone, but Israel needs the skill of an experienced guide! The advice of a reliable counselor stands alongside supernatural revelation! The wise will recognize that God affects his purpose through both methods: sometimes by miracles of direct intervention; but more often by ordinary good sense, linked with the use of the best available resources.

---

[219] That is, the cloud appears now to be responding to the forward march of Israel, rather than actively leading the way. This is confirmed by the LXX, which places verse 34 after verse 36.

Alison's Story

MORE PRAYERS ANSWERED (1981-1986)

A week later, while Ken was still in Singapore, I became extremely ill with a hemorrhage. When it had not stopped after three weeks, Sharon telephoned the doctor. He advised her, if the bleeding continued beyond another hour, she should bring me into Emergency. Instead, she decided to call a Christian friend, Dorothy Langstaff. God heard our prayers, and half an hour later the hemorrhage suddenly ended!

Ken's return from Singapore was a time of great rejoicing. We were about to experience our first Minneapolis winter, and it was good to know the head of the house was home. Our initiation into the mysteries of snow, icy roads, and frozen pipes was to begin with the worst winter Minnesota had suffered in 100 years!

One night Sharon went out to take a friend home. Because the car was warm, she neglected to take any heavy clothing with her. On her return journey she became lost in a fog. Unless she found a service station soon she would run out of fuel and maybe freeze to death by the side of the road. She prayed for guidance as she drove slowly along. Almost immediately she saw a gas station, and was able to fill up and return home safely. In our ignorance of the danger we had not been alarmed by her late arrival, but we praised God that we had taught our daughter to pray and seek guidance from him.

Since our arrival in the USA, six months earlier, three of us had faced a threat of death, and more was to come. Why was God allowing these things to happen?

I walked into our office one afternoon to find Ken in excruciating pain. He was doubled over and the perspiration was streaming down his face. I touched his forehead and it was cold, then almost at once he became extremely hot. "What is it," I cried.

"I've been having these bouts of pain for some time. I'm not sure what they are," he whispered.

"You must go to the doctor and have a check up. You owe it to your family!" I argued. It was frightening to see my strong husband in such pain. We prayed together and then made an appointment for him to see a physician.

The doctor's verdict was that the pain was caused either by cancer, gall stones, or an aneurism. A day was set for an x-ray. Meantime Ken was prayed for by two of his friends, Pastor Alan Langstaff and Pastor Rod Lensch. They agreed together that whatever was causing the pain would be healed. I was still full of apprehension. What would I do if Ken were to die? I prayed earnestly, but my mind was in a ferment could get no peace. God was unable to speak to me because I was unable to hear his voice. Then one morning, very early, I woke suddenly. This verse of scripture came into my mind, and I knew immediately that God was speaking to me - *"With long life will I satisfy him and show him my salvation"* (Psalm 91:16).

Immediately I knew Ken would live, that whatever had gripped him was undone. I had been given the faith of

God which nothing can shake!

Ken went in for his x-rays and the doctor was amazed, he could find nothing wrong. Quickly he took another x-ray and once again it showed nothing. This occurred nine years ago and he has had no more trouble since then.

LEARNING GOD'S PURPOSE

Now we had to face the fact that four of the family had had life threatening experiences in our first year in America. Why had this happened to us? Had we missed God's guidance? As we pondered the matter, we remembered that during our three years in Sydney we had not had to believe God for anything. Everything had come easily to us; consequently our "faith muscles" had grown very feeble. We could see plainly that God had now put us through a crash course. He needed to have us tough, and resilient in faith, not flaccid and weak. He had brought us through, as he always does when we trust him totally to keep us in his will.

The end of the two years arrived and, true to his word, the Lord gave us the opportunity to return to Australia. By that time however I was happy to stay. I realized that we had only begun to scratch the surface of the work that we had to do in upgrading and reediting the correspondence course for the American market.

Seven more years were to go by before we were to return to Australia, and before the last part of the verse God had given me in Tasmania was to be fulfilled. But that is another story, an unfinished one! God is in control and that is all we need to know.

Ninth Fallacy

"PROSPERITY SHOWS THAT I AM IN THE WILL OF GOD"

> When in disgrace with Fortune and men's eyes,
> I all alone beweepe my out-cast state,
> And trouble deafe heaven with my bootlesse cries, And look upon my self and curse my fate,
> Wishing me like to one more rich in hope,
> Featur'd like him, like him with friends possest,
> Desiring this man's art, and that man's skope,
> With what I most enjoy contented least;
> Yet in these thoughts my selfe almost despising, Haplye I thinke on thee - and then my state (Like to the Larke at breake of day arising From sullen earth) sings himns at Heaven's gate: For thy sweet love remember'd such wealth brings, That then I skorne to change my state with Kings.[220]

How well the poet understands the caprice of life, the pain of thwarted ambition, of crushed dreams, of disappointed hope. How easy it is to sink with him into envy of the higher art, the richer scope, of another person's skill! Who

---
[220] Shakespeare, Sonnet 29, original spelling.

has not been jealous of the greater success attained by a friend or neighbor? The poet almost reached the doleful state of despising even his own skills, the work of his hands he should most have enjoyed. In the end he discovered an abundant consolation in love, which turned his mournful sighs into laughter. Thoughts of his beloved lifted him with anthems of praise to the very gates of heaven.

The love he found, I suppose, was that of a true woman, and any man who has known such a priceless boon will share his paeans. The love of a devoted friend does indeed work the ancient alchemy of turning dross into gold. Beggars become kings when they love and are loved! And if human love should fail, then we may look higher, to the never-fading love of the Father.

Nonetheless, the poem presents one of life's bitterest dilemmas. Here is the hurt most people have to endure: their days do not turn out as they wish or expect. The noblest dreams of ordinary men and women are commonly and carelessly crushed by the pitiless tread of time. They need not purchase obscurity; it seizes them whether they wish it or not!

> *"Oblivion is not to be hired: the greater part must be content to be as though they had not been, to be found in the register of God, not in the record of man."*[221]

Nor are those who *do* fulfill their aspirations in any better state. For in the end all things on this planet are as ephemeral as a snowflake in the Sahara

---

[221] Sir Thomas Browne, Urn Burial ch. 5; A.D. 1658.

> The Wordly Hope men set their Hearts upon
> Turns Ashes - or it prospers; and anon,
> LikeSnow upon the Desert's dusty Face,
> Lighting a little hour or two - was gone.
> Think, in this batter'd Caravanserai
> Whose Portals are alternate Night and Day,
> How Sultan after Sultan with his Pomp
> Abode his destin'd Hour, and went his way.[222]

Surely you know by now that Christians are as much susceptible to the buffets and blows of this mindless world as are others? Pity then the person who measures his or her happiness or relationship with God, by the achievement of a high level of material prosperity. How swiftly their baubles can be snatched from them!

Solomon speaks of those whom either fortune or the providence of God had elevated from prison to a throne;[223] but he knows that the reverse may just as easily happen.

Who is bold enough to assert that no shadow will ever chill their happiness? I suppose some *are* so bold! But I tremble for them; for if sorrow does strike (as it probably will) how will they cope with it? As an Italian proverb says,

> *"It is too late to come with water when the house is burnt down."*

Those who are wise thatch their roof in the summertime,

---
[222] Omar Khayyam, op. cit., stanzas 17 & 18.
[223] Ecclesiastes 4:14.

before winter's damp falls on them. Sensible people get their faith, their spiritual resources, into good order before the day of trial fiercely dawns.

Yet the idea of life out of control still sits very uncomfortably in our minds. How much more appealing it is to think that God is fully in charge of even the smallest event. Surely there is a place of safety true believers can find from the perils that beset the ungodly?

Would that it were so! Unhappily it cannot be, because we live in;

A CAPRICIOUS WORLD

Following the 1989 earthquake in San Francisco, Robert McAfee Brown wrote -

> *"Life is capricious. That is the common thread in most of the stories told. `If I hadn't had to make that telephone call first ... ' or `If I hadn't been in the garden when the living room ceiling collapsed ... ' The unspoken conclusion to all of these conditional clauses is, `I'd be dead.'*

> *"In our soberest moments we already know that life is capricious: this one got AIDS, that one didn't; this one had a six-year remission from cancer, that one was dead in two months; this one got a seat on the plane that crashed because of a no-show just before departure time, that one arrived too late to get on. We can disregard the capriciousness of life most of the time, but after an earthquake it*

> *won't go away. We can extract this blessing from it: savor the moments you have before they disappear; appreciate relationships before they are lost; get that letter in the mail today; don't let the sun go down on your anger. Acknowledging capriciousness can also help us avoid trying to draw the divine design too neatly and coherently."*[224]

"Life is capricious," said Mr. Brown. We don't like the sound of that. We rest much more pleasantly with the thought of God firmly shaping everything that happens to us. Because the Lord sometimes miraculously rescues one of his servants, or because we have seen wonderful answers to prayer, we are quick to conclude that he never leaves anything to chance. We "disregard the capriciousness of life." That is not honest. It conforms neither to scripture nor experience. A careful person will not fall into the trap of "trying to draw the divine plan too neatly and coherently."

That is our problem. We yearn to bring order into disorder, to remove hazard from the events of each day. We feel driven to fit God's actions into a lucid pattern, to compel his works (or lack of them) to conform to a scheme that makes sense to us. Especially, we feel obliged to show that nice things happen to nice people, and only the nasty suffer hurt. At least, we want to prove that the Lord does take special care of the righteous.

The attempt is not wholly wrong. Anyone with a concordance can find scores of biblical statements that health and prosperity are the boon of godly faith. Across

---

[224] From an article, On Earthquakes and Aftershocks, in "The Christian Century", November 15, 1989; pg. 1039.

the whole church, and over many years, those promises show a bountiful fulfillment. Good people do eventually triumph over evil.

Consider, for example, the American Wild West. It provides a paradigm of the growth of every culture. Shopkeepers and bankers, merchants and clerks, schoolteachers and physicians, lawyers and clergymen, finally proved tougher than gunslingers. Frontier towns were tamed. Schools and churches replaced saloons and bordellos. The growing communities flourished in peace and prosperity.

Yet violence continues; crime is not wholly eradicated from the cattle country; nature remains harsh. Some of those now gentle towns will again be torn by riot; others may be ravaged by famine or flood, earthquake or fire. No community can be sure that tomorrow will bring only greater happiness and wealth.

The same is true for individual Christians. The taming of sin brings new dimensions of health and prosperity into their lives. The gospel does lift people to higher levels of culture and achievement. But no guarantee exists to assure any one person a life free from trouble and heartbreak. On the contrary, Jesus himself taught that we are all subject to:

THE VAGARIES OF LIFE

Christ found an example of life's mystery in a collapsing tower that crushed some innocent bystanders, while others escaped. He also told how Pilate's thugs once butchered a group of worshippers in the temple, while others were left unscathed.[225] The disciples were puzzled. How could God allow such things to happen in front of his very altar? Why didn't he protect those praying people? If you are not safe in church, where can you hope to find safety? Jesus gave no explanation.[226] To ask the question was foolish; to attempt an answer, more foolish.

The disciples supposed that the people who were crushed or murdered must have been guilty of unbelief, or of some dread sin. No! Jesus scorned such crass and futile judgments. He left the tragic complexities of life unexplained. He saw what anyone with an open eye must see: a day sometimes brings good, and sometimes evil. The passing hours show little regard for the character of people when they dispense their dispassionate dole. Is there then nothing to learn from the hurts that beset some people but not others? How foolish! Even in the blackest night two precious gifts lie waiting: a warning to be ready; a grace to be received -

BE READY!

Since each day is so uncertain, said Jesus and since none

---

[225] Luke 13:1-5; and cp. Matthew 5:45.

[226] Luke can be updated by a couple of millennia. For example, within a recent two-year span in southern California, armed gunmen burst into three different churches, during worship services, shooting and killing seven people and wounding six. Why these churches and no others? Why these people and no others? Those who died lacked even the honor of bravely yielding their lives as martyrs to the faith. They were killed suddenly, for no good reason, during spasms of pathological social violence. One of the newspaper reports contained this paragraph: "A man shot and killed a pastor and deacon in a Baptist church in Los Angeles' Chinatown. The killer was then shot to death by a sheriff's deputy who had been attending the service." Were that pastor and deacon special sinners? How callow! They were simply unfortunate victims of one man's deranged hatred.

of us can know what the hour will bring,[227] we should live before God in a state of sincere repentance. Keep a tender conscience! Keep a gentle spirit! Who can tell'? You or I may be the next to perish on the freeway; we ourselves may be assaulted in our homes, or even in church!

Of course, the reverse is equally true. Be ready also for a miracle, for tomorrow may bring a marvelous surprise from the Father, some joyful intervention, some happy largesse, given to fill your hours with rapture. Those happy boons, indeed, are more likely to be your portion than some sorrowful bane. Beyond question, the thrust of scripture is toward a promise of well-being and good success for the people of God. Everywhere we are taught to pray for just such a glad result to crown each day's trustful living.

For example, just last night Alison and I had planned to meet two friends and go with them to hear a full performance of Handel's "Messiah". We were looking forward to the evening with keen pleasure, but through various mix-ups we didn't meet our friends at the arranged time. We drove from place to place looking for them for an hour, and were just about to give up when suddenly a horn sounded. There, in the car immediately behind us, were our friends! It was peak-traffic time. Thousands of vehicles thronged the highways. The odds against our two cars coming so precisely together were astronomical! If we had tried to arrange such an encounter we could not have achieved it. We felt the kindly hand of the Father, granting us a small pearl of joy.

---

[227] Compare James 4:13-15.

Alison and I have had many such sweet gifts from heaven across the years; some as inconsequential as that meeting on the freeway, others profoundly important. I could fill this entire book with stories of answered prayer, both great and small.

Yet there is no steady pattern. I have missed appointments much more necessary than one for a concert. Why didn't God help me then, when his help would have been even more welcome? What about those occasions when Alison and I desperately needed a miracle; but it did not come? Heaven was silent, the hand of God was still - or God chose to answer our prayer in another way, perhaps giving us strength to struggle on against seemingly insuperable hardship. We were like Jesus, who in one place confidently declared that the Father always heard him;[228] yet later when he most yearned for God to rescue him, found that his plea was rejected.[229] Still he yielded to the Father's will, embraced the cross, and found a nobler triumph than his first prayer could have brought him.

The longer I live, and pray, and expect great things from the Father, the more I realize that God sets his own pace and his own program! He declines to consult my schedule; he does not march to the beat of my drum! He steadily insists that I should echo the prayer of the Master: "Not my will, O Lord, but thine be done!" which includes God choosing to do nothing at all, when he might

---

[228] John 11:41-42.
[229] Luke 22:41-44. I have never wanted anything from God so desperately as Jesus craved the removal of that "cup". Yet Christ had to accept the Father's "no". What was the "cup"? We are not told. It certainly was not a fear of death (cp. Matthew 10:28; Luke 6:22-23). Perhaps for the first time he was becoming fully aware of how totally he had to be identified with human sin at the cross - there is a terrible mystery in the words, "he was made sin for us" (2 Corinthians 5:21).

do everything!

ACCIDENTS HAPPEN!

But surely (someone protests), if I learn how to believe the promises of God, how to wax bold in faith, can I not travel through life unharmed? Can I not sidestep danger, smooth out irregularities, avoid everything God has not chosen?

If you listen to Jesus you will change your mind.

He refused to say that a little more faith would have protected those temple-goers from Pilate's assassins. Nor did he allow that a closer walk with God would have kept those unfortunate bystanders away from the falling tower. They were all victims of circumstances over which they had
no control; ordinary people, overtaken by mishaps they could not avoid.[230]

I have encountered the same:

- some families were driving home from a prayer meeting, over a high bridge. Most of them reached the other side safely. But then a

---

[230] Someone might point to Luke 10:19 ("nothing shall by any means hurt you"), and similar passages. Do they not promise a high level of divine protection? Yes, they do, a very high level, much higher than mere earthly safety! Given the frequent violence, the perils, the savage death, which overtook many of the apostles, Jesus obviously was not promising them any immunity from pain in this life. Christ intended his words to be applied more deeply, to spiritual safety, to a secure heritage in the kingdom, to heavenly treasures that no foe, whether demonic or human, can ever steal. In a less absolute sense, the promise of Luke 10:19 may be applicable to this life - especially in relation to the healing covenant; but its fullest guarantee belongs not to the temporal but to the eternal realm.

cargo ship hit the centre span, causing a section of the roadway to fall into the river. Unable to stop in time, several cars plunged over the edge, two hundred feet to the water below. The occupants all perished.

Among those who died were people who had been to the prayer meeting. Were they less trusting, less righteous, less loved by God than those who got home without harm? Did God plan their terrifying and untimely deaths to fulfill some hidden purpose? The idea is almost blasphemous.

- after I had dismissed a Bible college class, the students drove off to their various destinations. But one of them never arrived. He was killed at a highway intersection. Was he more sinful than the others, or weaker in his faith? Some of his fellow students suggested as much. They gained only my indignant rebuke.
- another Bible college student was paying his way through school by working as a builder's laborer on a ten-storey building. A lift operator mistook his signal, and instead of raising the platform, suddenly released it. The young man tumbled through a hundred feet of steel girders. When he struck the ground he was battered almost past recognition, and had to be kept unconscious until he died a few days later.

Was that the devil's work, or God's judgment? Both suggestions are repugnant. It was just a terrible accident, which left a young wife and mother of two children bereft of her deeply loved husband.

- a family from my church, after attending worship in the morning, went for a Sunday afternoon drive into the country. On the way back, another vehicle crowded with drunken teenagers struck their car. The young people all survived. The Christian family was destroyed, except for one little girl who was left orphaned and crippled for life.

Does the Lord care more for the ungodly than for his own children? Or was the collision just a result of the peril we all face on the road?

- three children were playing in a park close to their homes. A stranger approached, pulled out a pistol, and compelled one of them, an eleven-year old boy, to go with him. The boy was never seen again. His parents are Christians; the parents of the other children were not. Who can imagine the anguish, the months of distraught terror, suffered by the family whose child was taken? In vain they cried out to God to help them locate their son. The child remains unfound, his fate unknown. In church one day the parents suffer further torment, when an elderly lady happily tells how God helped her to find a precious book she had lost.

Does God care more about a book than a boy? Why did he respond to her tears, but not to theirs? They wonder if they will ever come out of the abyss of pain and doubt into which they have plunged.[231]

What can you say to such dire sorrows? What rational explanation can you give for events so brutally mindless? To people so shattered and bereft, how can you justify the actions of God?

Jesus repudiated such questions. Since they have no final answer this side of the resurrection, why ask them? Possibly the devil was to blame; possibly (in some cases) even the hand of God was involved. Who can tell? More probably, all those unhappy people were like the victims of the collapsing tower: simply unfortunate enough to be in a certain place at the wrong time. They could have been somewhere else; but by their own innocent choice they were found in a place of death.

Of course, it is just as easy to multiply examples of divine deliverance. I could tell about the miracles of healing God has given my family, and about amazing experiences of divine supply. We could rejoice together about those occasions when all hope seemed lost, until suddenly the Lord spoke light into the darkness. Chains snapped apart, prison doors swung open, provision poured out of heaven. An angel could hardly count the number of times God has extricated his children from danger and showered his goodness upon them.

Yet even if you can look back (as Alison and I can), and see many times when your life has been incredibly spared, still you have no promise that it will be spared again. You and I have no more guarantee of perpetual safety than others had who have perished. So be ready to meet your

---

[231] The above incidents are all based on actual events.

God - not tomorrow, but today![232]

RICHES OF GRACE

Is there then no difference between us and the ungodly? Of course there is! Our case is never the same as theirs. No matter what happens to us, or is happening around us, we always have a mighty resource in the Lord God himself. His grace, strength, wisdom, stand freely available, always more than sufficient, either to deliver us from danger, or despite it to keep us victorious.[233]

We are like Shadrach, Meshach, and Abednego. Faced with Nebuchadnezzar's "fiery furnace', they stood unbowed, confident God was with them. They knew he would either liberate them from the furnace, bring them unscathed through it, or, if they were to die, give them courage and victory over death.[234] For us, too the Fourth Man is always there in the flames! We are never alone!

Those three young men were pulled out of the furnace, not even singed by its heat. But suppose the flames had prevailed - as they have over many other martyrs who were just as strong in faith would that have made any difference? Of course not. Whether alive or dead, Shadrach and his friends remain heroes, their resurrection into eternal life assured, their destiny in the kingdom fixed. That is why the writer to the Hebrews could talk about two strikingly different groups of spiritual champions. Some by a miracle dulled a lion's hunger, quenched fire, turned back the sword, or gained a throne. Others gladly yielded themselves to loneliness,

---

[232] Compare Amos 4:12.
[233] 2 Corinthians 12:8-9; 8:9; Psalm 23:4.
[234] Daniel 3:16-18.

thirst, or to an unspeakable death. Yet they too were giants of faith, unswerving in their allegiance to their God.[235]

Let it be said again and again: for us, who believe in Christ, there is no defeat. It is impossible for any man or woman who refuses to let go of Jesus to be finally overcome by wickedness or death. We are destined for triumph! We never can doubt the ultimate goodness of God's providence. We know that in the end, all will be well. We are committed to a cause beyond ourselves, serving a goal beyond our own self-interest. A loftier vision than mere personal happiness engrosses our soul, and turns all despair into unconquerable hope -

> "Rise, soul, from thy despairing knees!
> What if thy lips have drunk the lees?
> Fling forth thy sorrows to the wind
> And link thy hope with humankind
> The passion of a larger claim
> Will put thy puny grief to shame!"[236]

FAITH IS NEEDED

This all suggests that God works more often unseen than seen. He prefers background action above foreground, the hidden above the overt. Thus, in war, some church properties stand miraculously preserved, while others become heaps of rubble. On the freeway, an angel may protect one Christian family, while another is obliterated

---

[235] Hebrews 11:32-39.
[236] Angela Morgan, Today, last stanza. She suggests that the "larger claim" to which we should be committed is the welfare of the whole human race. That is a noble goal, but not high enough. Paul expressed a better aim: "I am straining toward the prize of the upward call of God in Christ Jesus" (Philippians 3:14).

in a fatal accident. One man testifies how God miraculously prevented him from boarding a plane that crashed; yet in the same disaster another Christian died. Sometimes the home or business of an ungodly man withstands a gale, while that of a godly family collapses.

When I hear people telling how amazingly the Lord has delivered them from sure death or ruin, I rejoice with them, and praise the Father for his goodness. Scripture itself says we should give thanks to God in every circumstance, and to let our joy abound more and more.[237] Yet sometimes those testimonies are offensively glib. What about the hapless people who did not survive? Did the Lord have no care for them?

Alison recently read to me an account about a Christian engineer's amazing rescue. The hero described a long sequence of events that made him too late to board a ship. He went back home exasperated and angry, until he learned that soon after leaving port the ship had exploded and sank. There were no survivors. The engineer at once thanked God for arranging his late arrival at the terminal, and thus sparing his life. He also quickly repented of the chagrin he had felt when he watched the vessel sail away. Heartily he praised the Lord for a miracle of preservation, which of course was the correct thing for him to do.

Yet in the entire account not one word of sympathy was expressed for the scores of passengers and seamen who had perished in the accident. I listened in vain for any hint of the mystery surrounding one man's preservation while many others met violent death. Were there no other

---

[237] Philippians 4:4-6; plus many other references.

Christians on that ship? Was the engineer really prevented from getting there on time by the hand of God? If it was God, why was this man the only one so spared?

Perhaps he was right; perhaps his life had been preserved by God's personal intervention. But how could he know that? In any case, less certainty about himself, and more pity for those who had died so wretchedly, would have made his story more impressive to me. As it was, I felt more offended than inspired.

JOB AND THE WHIRLWIND

The saga of Job raises the same quandary. Despite the facile reasons often given for the disasters that overwhelmed Job,[238] the book itself is silent on the matter. When the Lord finally appeared to the patriarch in a whirlwind, he offered no explanation for the calamities that had struck Job and his family. Nor did any vindication of divine justice come out of the tumultuous blast. God gave Job only one thing: a vision of

---

[238] I mean, of course, some fault in the patriarch himself. Such as: he had yielded himself to fear; he was self-righteous; he was proud and stubborn; and the like. The Prologue suggests that God made us of Job's pain to demonstrate righteousness to Satan, but no blame is attached to Job. All attempts to pin some sin onto him founder on a rocky blasphemy. They presuppose that God was willing to cause, or at least allow, the violent and undeserved deaths of many other people (1:13-Continued from page 165...19) just to teach one favored man a spiritual lesson. Apart from the fact that Satan was the actual agent of destruction, the book nowhere tells us why such miseries fell on Job. Even if it is allowed that Job was fearful, proud, self-righteous, and the like (which he may have been), the problem remains. Why did his sins (which at their worst were mild, 31:1-40) bring such a horrible penalty? Many others have committed far worse crimes, yet have lived out their days in good health and affluence. His own friends were just as guilty as Job, yet escaped affliction. In the end we are driven to conclude: there is no satisfying explanation of why he suffered and not his friends; nor why Job was spared, while his sons, daughters, and servants were killed without opportunity to repent or build a new life. Our only answer is the anguish God himself embraced at Calvary, and the endless life and joy promised in Christ's resurrection.

divine glory.[239] Even that was severely limited; for Job saw nothing of heaven, but only the splendors of the physical creation. Yet it was enough. The patriarch got no answers, but he did lose his questions![240] One glimpse of the majesty of the Most High made him speechless. The mystery remained, but Job was satisfied.

William Safire, the renowned columnist, moved by disappointment at the untimely death of the great Russian human rights activist, Andrei Sakharov, made this comment on the ironies of history -

> *"A deeper question arises: what kind of justice blesses tyrants like Pol Pot, Castro, and Ceausescu[241] with longevity, while a crusader for freedom is snatched away at the crucial moment? That issue of the suffering of the sinless was raised by the near-heretical poet who wrote the Book of Job, and answered with a refutation of the pious notion of divine retribution. Don't look to God for justice; life is unfair. Cherish instead the God-given right to challenge unjust authority".[242]*

'Life is unfair!" Those words scrape us unpleasantly, but can you deny them? Not with any reason or truth. Yet people who crave, as Job's friends did, predictable

---

[239] Job 38:1-4, ff.
[240] Job 40:1-3; 42:1-4.
[241] After 24 years of dictatorship in Romania, Ceausescu was driven from power by a popular uprising, and put to death by firing squad on Christmas day, 1989.
[242] From a report from Washington, published in The San Diego Union, December 18th, 1989. Think also about the stories of Israel's kings, found in the Old Testament. One of the most wicked of Judah's monarchs, Manasseh, sat upon the throne the longest (55 years), while some of the godly kings were cut off in the prime of life. No clear relationship can be established between godliness and the length of reign, or even the prosperity, of the kings.

consistency in the actions of Providence, are secretly promoting just such a denial. They hope to smooth out life's inequalities, or at least to make the insane seem sane. "*Good things,'* they argue, *"happen only to good people; bad things happen only to bad people.*" Thus they hope to give coherence to a horribly incoherent world; to provide an emotionally satisfying explanation for the wrenching disparities that exist in society. Their ilk can be found everywhere in the church. The lesson of Job remains largely unlearned.

Job himself, however, understood well what God was trying to teach him. His encounter with the whirlwind left him content to place his life at the Lord's disposal. Calm trust replaced querulous complaint. It so happened that his fortunes were restored; but that was incidental. Suppose instead he had died on the ash heap. Would that have altered the message of the book? Not in the slightest. Job had discovered that whether he gained riches or lost them, kept or departed this life, achieved his worldly goals or failed them, he had only one true treasure: on the last day he would be clothed in the glory of God. He had mastered the truth later expressed by Paul -

> *"whatever my circumstances, I have learned to rest easy. I am no stranger to poverty; yet I have also handled riches. I know the secret of how to be content, no matter what is happening to me or around me. So whether I am eating well or going hungry, whether enjoying wealth or suffering want, I am more than able to cope with it. Christ himself is the one who infuses me with this abundant inner*

strength."[243]

RENOUNCE FATALISM

"I don't understand," someone may be saying. "The opening lines of your book stress the importance of believing that God is in control, that he has a plan for my life, that he orders my daily affairs, and is willing to answer prayer miraculously. Now you seem to be reducing Christian life to a passive submission to indifferent fate."

Well, perhaps you are not saying that. In fact, if you have been reading carefully you could not say it. Surely I have stated clearly enough that most Christians do enjoy each day good things from the Father's hand.

Yet despite the false assurance aroused by popular piety, we have to admit a tension between the promise of divine superintendence and the realities observed both in scripture and in life. The common experience of many is not necessarily the case with each person.

I hope you will be among those whose days are rich with heaven's bounty. Like John, I heartily "wish above all things that you may prosper and be in health, even as your soul prospers." Yet it may not be so - at least, not in the ordinary, worldly, material sense of the prayer - for you may be among those who must seek their consolation in Christ, and their miracle, on a higher level - as indeed, ultimately, we all must. For heaven, not earth, eternity, not time, is the final goal of every promise of God.

Fatalism, therefore, a helpless resignation to the

---

[243] Philippians 4:11-13.

inevitable, should never be part of Christian thinking. No matter what is happening to you, or around you, there is always room for a miracle, there is always some grace to receive from God. The redemptive power of Christ is built into every experience; out of every event the believer can draw riches to lodge in the heavenlies. From every occurrence some honor can be gained for Christ; in every situation some victory can be won in his name. We are never without resources. The Father never abandons his children. If their prayers cannot be answered in one way, they will be answered in another. If God chooses not to prevent wickedness or harm, he will manifest his sovereignty all the more mightily in over-ruling their effects. He makes the worst violence of demons or men work his higher will. Whatever the thief steals in time, the Father will return without measure in eternity.

So whichever way you look at it, we Christians cannot lose! We are only winners!

Alison's Story

BACK TO AUSTRALIA! (1990-)

"God, please tell us what to do and we'll do it. Whatever it is!"

This was an exasperated cry from the bottom of my heart. I was truly frustrated and bewildered.

It was around July 1989. For months we had been praying for guidance as to what God wanted us to do next. Our house was on the market but not selling. Ministry opportunities had dried up. We felt as though we were in a cocoon of silence. We couldn't reach others and they were, seemingly, ignoring us.

Pastors and churches which normally were only too eager for Ken's ministry were strangely silent. We waited on God. Weeks went by, finally, in sheer frustration I decided to get a nursing job, which I did.

More time elapsed.

Meanwhile, Ken finished writing his book, "when the Trumpet Sounds' and began writing a book on guidance - this book, *Discovery*.

How did we get ourselves into this position? We had resigned from our church in San Diego, feeling our time there was ended. We had been confident that we would receive plenty of itinerant ministries to keep us going.

But, nothing, silence from everyone, and what was far worse, silence from God.

Every other time in our lives we had been fully confident of our next step but this time, NOTHING! Hence my cry, "Tell us what to do!"

Then in September I received word that my mother had had a stroke, and of course I made plans to visit her in Australia. While there, I was amazed at the number of pastors and leaders who were anxious for Ken to return to Australia. We had thought there was no place for us in Australia; because we had been gone so long, we were no longer needed. I mentioned this to Ken on the telephone and he prayed about it and after a week of waiting on God, made the decision to return.

After nine months of stagnation as far as selling our house was concerned, that very week we had a buyer who made us an acceptable offer on the house.

Was God waiting for us to make the decision to return to Australia? Had he shown us that is what he wanted but we hadn't listened?

Whatever the reason, the experience certainly gave us some new views on guidance, which have become a great blessing to many people.

Is it possible that God was giving us the option to stay in U.S.A. or leave for Australia? Perhaps he was; but I think he did want us to return to Australia for three reasons:

first: he had given me a scripture years before that we would return to our homeland. Then

second: he had caused ministry to dry up for us in the U.S.A. (Invitations to return to the U.S.A. began to come in immediately we returned to Australia. If we had had those invitations before we left we would have stayed in the U.S.A.). And

third: God opened up the hearts of the people of Penrith Christian Fellowship Centre to take care of us. Without their invitation and offer of housing and transport we could not have returned to Australia.

So we came back to our home country early in 1990. Since then, new ministry opportunities have opened to us abundantly, both in Australia and overseas. Indeed, we have never before enjoyed ministry so much as we are now, nor has our ministry together ever been more fruitful. So in the end the guiding hand of our Lord proved sure and certain. As David discovered, the Shepherd's way may sometimes lead into a dark and dismal valley, in which death threatens, but he will never abandon us there to perish. Rather, his rod and staff retain firm control, and with sure steps he brings his sheep through the valley, into his promised pasture.

Tenth Fallacy

"TRUE FAITH IS CONTENT TO STEP INTO THE DARK!"

> Lead, kindly Light, amid the encircling
>   gloom;
> Lead thou me on!
> The night is dark, and I am far from
>   home;
> Lead thou me on!
> Keep thou my feet: I do not ask to see
>   The distant scene; one step enough
>   for me.[244]

The familiar words soothe us. They reach deep into our spirits and stir recognition of truth. We do not need to know tomorrow; it is enough that the Father's hand carries us along today. His light shines in the darkness, and we follow it with joy.

But something is not quite right. True, there may be days when we can do nothing else but stumble along, straining to follow a glimmer of divine illumination. Yet to make such a quiescent approach a total rule of life is too passive. Think about Jesus and other great leaders in the Bible, who knew the call of God, who had vision and

---

[244] John Henry, Cardinal Newman (1801-1890).

direction, who fixed their faith upon reaching goals that were clearly set before them. They did not step blindly into the dark. They knew where they were going and intended to get there!

A CHAMELEON DEITY?

How sharply that firm purpose opposes those who cannot take a step without hunting for a "word" from God. Yet true growth in wisdom seems to be better demonstrated, not by an *increasing* frequency of "words" from heaven, but by a *decreasing* need for them. I see scant reason to admire those "pious" and "spiritual" people who boast how often they hear from God, how clearly he speaks to them, how closely he controls their daily lives. They constantly announce, "The Lord told me to do this, or that, or to go here, or there."

Sturdy skepticism is the best response to such doubtful claims.

I have also noticed this: the more frequently a person claims to be led by God, the more often the Lord seems to change his mind! Here is a pious soul (like the young man in an earlier chapter) who yesterday was sure God had told him to do a thing; but today (he says) the Lord is telling him something different. Not only different, but *against* his previous instruction! Truly, people who want to be constantly directed by the Spirit need short memories, otherwise they become completely confused! Or perhaps, as Solomon warned, they just get angry with God.[245] I have met all three types: those who have a wonderful capacity to forget yesterday's instruction when

---

[245] Proverbs 19:3, "A man wrecks his life by his own stupidity, and then he wants to blame God for it!"

they receive today's "revelation"; those who sit bewildered because their "guidance" brought disaster; and those who are furious with God for deceiving them!

The chameleon deity worshipped by those misguided souls is not *my* God. The true Lord of Heaven is constant in his purpose, sure in his promise, firm in his wisdom, trustworthy in all his ways. Leave that other changeling god to the heathen, who revel in vacillatory oracles and capricious spirits. Although even among pagans, the wise ridiculed their fellows whose lives were controlled hourly by portents of various kinds

> *"The superstitious man is the kind of person who during the day would walk around only after he had washed his hands and sprinkled himself,[246] and after he had taken into his mouth a bit of laurel from the sanctuary. If a weasel runs across the road, he does not proceed until someone else goes by, or until he throws three stones across the road.... If a mouse eats through a sack of barley meal, he goes to the exegete to ask what he should do. If the exegete[247] tells him to give the sack to a saddler to stitch up, he does not heed this (sensible and practical) advice, but goes away and performs expiation's. If owls hoot at him as he is walking along, he is thrown into a dither and continues on only after he has said, `Athena in mightier!'*[248] *And he does not*

---

[246] Thus fulfilling certain religious rituals, by which he hoped to attract the favor of the gods, just as some naïve Christians do today.
[247] An expert in interpreting both "signs" and religious lore.
[248] Just like some Christians, who have their own variety of sayings by which they hope to ward off evil. They depend on saying exactly the right words, instead of simply trusting God.

step on a tomb, nor is he willing to pay his respects to a dead man or to a woman after childbirth. He says that it is better for him not to become polluted.

"... And when he has a dream, he goes to the dream-interpreter, to the soothsayers, and to the bird-watchers, to ask to which god or goddess he ought to pray.... And if he sees a madman or an epileptic, he shudders and spits into his pockets."[249]

I have met Christians who are just as superstitious as that foolish Greek. They endlessly look for hidden significance in the ordinary events of life; nothing can happen but they are sure a secret message from God is threaded into it. The unreliable voice heard by those Christian omen-seekers sounds to me more like a tricky incubus than the constant Author of all Truth and Light.

We should aim instead for a dependable understanding of God's purpose. Build your guidance, not upon an endless succession of omens, signs, and "words", but upon a deep perception of the divine will, wrought out of scripture and prayer.

The manner in which God wants to bring us from that lower spiritual plane to a higher, can be illustrated by

THE URIM AND THUMMIN

When the Lord God first brought Israel out of Egypt the

---

[249] The speaker is Theophrastus, a 4th. cent. B.C. Greek philosopher, in his "Characters" ch. 16 (a study of various moral types). Taken from Athenian Popular Religion, by J. D. Mikalson; University of North Carolina Press, 1983; pg. 46-47; (brackets mine).

people were like little children, needing clear guidance. So in the wilderness he gave them the fiery cloud, and then the *"Urim and Thummin"*.[250]

The latter was a means of obtaining supernatural direction from God by "yes" or "no" answers to questions asked by the priest. How this was done is unknown, although it may have been two stones, black on one side and white on the other, that were cast into a priest's lap. Two white faces meant "yes"; two black faces "no"; one black, and one white, "wait", or "perhaps". Anyhow, the early Israelites thought this mysterious practice was an easy and practical means of learning heaven's will.

However, by the time the separate kingdoms of Israel and Judah were established, use of the Urim and Thummin had already begun to dwindle. As the people matured in their faith, they gradually sought higher and nobler ways of ascertaining the mind of God. Divinatory practices seemed too redolent of superstition and too much like pagan methods.

So devout citizens turned instead to a growing dependence upon the written word. The colored stones were pushed aside, until they became just a memory. After the Jews returned from their exile in Babylon, the Urim was never again used. It had vanished completely from the national life.

Sirach provides a dramatic demonstration of this change. He does not hesitate to declare his admiration of Aaron and the priestly oracles -

---

[250] Exodus 28:30; Numbers 27:21; 1 Samuel 28:6; etc., including many places where it simply says that Israel, or some leader, "enquired of the Lord;" cp. 1 Samuel 14:36-42.

> *"Let us now praise famous men, and our fathers in their generations ... (God) highly honored Aaron (and) clothed him with ... a holy garment, rich with gold, blue, and purple, skillfully wrought by an embroiderer. With him was the oracle of righteousness, the Urim and <u>Thummin</u>"*[251]

But then Sirach plainly stated his preference for the written law *above the sacred* oracle

> *"The man who fears the Lord is safe from any threat of evil; for the Lord will rescue him out of every time of trouble. No wise man will ever scorn the law; but anyone who handles it deceitfully will be tossed about like a ship in a storm. Those who trust in the law will be given understanding; they will find the law more dependable than the <u>divine oracle</u>* (the Urim and Thummin)."[252]

Sirach could hardly denounce the little pebbles. They had, after all, been given to Israel by God himself. Yet the rabbi makes his preference clear: the written word was far more reliable than those rattling stones. A priest's lap might conjure a doubtful message; but absolute trust could be placed in scripture.

The same process - moving from divination to scripture - is shown in the development of the prophets away from immediate "words" addressed to particular situations (which characterized, say, an Elijah), to the broad concepts of righteousness, justice, mercy, which exemplify

---

[251] Sirach 44:1; 45:6,10.
[252] Sirach 33:1-3

the later prophets.

For example, as great as Elijah was, his influence cannot begin to equal that of an Isaiah or Jeremiah. The "writing" prophets have had a vastly greater impact upon the world than the "miracle" prophets.[253] I do not mean to disparage Elijah. He was a man of his time, and reached his generation in the best way possible. But as the people matured in their understanding they looked past physical augurs to a higher vision of the glory of God.

If a graph were drawn of that ascending spirituality, what point on it would you occupy? I hope you have grown past the need for things like pebbles to help you find the will of God. The Word and the Spirit working together within a framework of obedient faith are enough to hold any believer on the way of righteousness.

DRAWING A BOUNDARY

> *"I strongly urged Apollos to visit you with the other brethren, but it was not at all his will to come now. He will come when he has opportunity."*[254]

Where is there any suggestion of a need to obtain supernatural guidance on the matter? Paul felt Apollos should go; Apollos disagreed; the matter was left for Apollos to decide.

Here is the main point: where should you place a boundary to define the usual limits of divine involvement

---

[253] Not that God is any less willing today to work miracles than he was in Elijah's time. His signs and wonders are still abundant for those who believe; Mark 16:15-20. The issue is simply where your primary trust is located: in the actions of God, or in his word.
[254] 1 Corinthians 16:12.

in your life? Up to this boundary, you would not normally expect the Lord to intervene in your decisions. Beyond this boundary, you would expect, and need, much more divine intervention. Every Christian sets such a crossover, either consciously or unconsciously.

Some draw the borderline very close - like a man I heard once, who said he depended upon God to choose even the restaurant at which he ate. Further, if he were to go into a restaurant to order beef, and found only chicken there, he would conclude that God did not want him to eat beef that day; however, it must be important for him to eat chicken!

Surely such a narrow outlook trivializes Christian life, and reduces it to absurdity. cannot imagine finding it necessary to ask God's permission, before deciding whether to eat here or there, or the like. How bizarre!

Others (myself among them) usually place the line much further away, while allowing there are times when God wants to control even the particulars of an event. Yet those occasions seem rare. You must decide for yourself where to draw the boundary most appropriately in your own life. A main purpose of this book is to help you make that decision wisely.

CONCLUSION

NO FINAL GUARANTEES

What shall we say to these things?

A first reaction must be: there is no fixed or final method for gaining infallible guidance; yet a combination of several of the principles discussed in this book can be trusted to keep you walking on the right path most of the time. The more important the decision, the more factors you should try to bring together before finally committing yourself.

Therefore, make use of all the resources God has put in your hands -

>   his word
>   prayer
>   good counsel
>   personal experience
>   your circumstances
>   spiritual revelation
>   common sense
>   - and the like.

Yet none of those tools guarantee infallible guidance; none of them are perfect for determining what you should do in every situation. You will be safest when you look for as broad a combination of them as possible.

Even then you will sometimes be mistaken. As Winston Churchill said when he had forgotten something he should have remembered, "all great men make mistakes". We might write ourselves also into Churchill's depiction of the Poles: "There are few virtues they do not possess – and there are few mistakes they have ever avoided!"[255] That doesn't matter. We learn by our mistakes. The dark valleys of life teach us wisdom, and also the green pastures.

These things all show us that we must

LEARN TO LIVE WITH MYSTERY

> *"Negative Capability, that is, when a man is capable of being in uncertanties, mysteries, doubts, without any irritable reaching after fact and reason."*[256]

People who cannot endure mystery must either adopt an ostrich-like refusal to see the obvious, or lapse inot bewildered dismay, "irritably reaching for", demanding, clear answers to every problem. But some questions have no answers; some tragedies defy explanation. We must be willing, this side of the grave, to allow darkness to shroud a part of life. We have not yet come to that time when

> *"there will be no more death and mourning; nor will there be any more suffering or tears ... Never again will there be any night"*[257]

When the great 19th century American preacher and orator, Henry Ward Beecher, lay dying, his last words were, *"Now comes the mystery."* That hardly seems right. Surely beyond the grave is the very place we will find clarity! If you do not believe that you do not believe

---

[255] From a speech in the House of Commons, August 16th, 1945.
[256] John Keats, English poet (1795-1821), from one of his letters.
[257] Revelation 21:3-4; 22:5.

scripture. *This* side of heaven, not *that*, is the place of mystery. Here is where perplexity haunts us -

"In the deepest heart of all of us there is a corner in which the ultimate mystery of things works sadly."[258]

When Alison and I were in Edinburgh, we visited Holy Rood palace, the residence of the Queen when she visits Scotland officially. Among many fascinating things hanging on the castle walls were several magnificent tapestries, some of them ancient, and large enough to carpet a floor. I suppose they were priceless. We tarried as long as we could, admire them, and meditating on the now-vanished way of life they depicted. remembered also an illustration a preacher told many years ago. He said that life is like a tapestry; it makes sense, it shows design and purpose, only when the weaver's task is done. That is because (he said) the weaver works from the back of the tapestry, not its front. If you inspect the cloth while it is still on the loom, you will see only a tangled mass of threads. But when the master-artist has completed his work, and the cloth is turned over, behold the beauty his unerring hand and eye have wrought!

Thus your life may seem to be a meaningless jumble of disconnected events, haphazard, ludicrous, perhaps tragic. But at the end of the journey, after the resurrection, standing at the Father's throne, the mystery will be resolved, and the loveliness the hand of God has wrought will be evident to every onlooker. At present our sight is murky at best; but then we shall see clearly and

---

[258] William James, American philosopher (1842-1910), The Will to Believe: Is Life Worth Living? (1897).

understand with joy![259]

The same idea is captured in these lines handed to me by a dear friend, Elizabeth Thornton, who found them many years ago in her father's Bible, after his death -

> Not till the Loom is silent,
> And the shuttles cease to fly,
> Shall God unroll the canvas
> And explain the reason, why
> The dark threads were as needful
> In the Weaver's skilful hand,
> As the threads of gold and silver
> For the pattern that he planned.[260]

REACH FOR MATURITY

Your highest quest, then, should be to arrive at a state of spiritual maturity, of fusion with the mind and heart of God, when your choices will naturally reflect what God wants. Then of your own volition you will walk in the path the Father has chosen for you. You may not understand why he chooses this way, or that, but you will be content to trust his benevolent wisdom.

Nonetheless, you will face some crossroads where nothing less than a direct miracle of guidance will be enough to show you the way. So always be ready for God to

---

[259] 1 Corinthians 13:12.

[260] Just a few days after writing the above paragraph, while reading a book of poetry, I unexpectedly came across the full poem from which the quoted lines were taken. They comprise the last two stanzas of a seven-stanza poem called The Loom of Time. The author is apparently unknown. The first stanza reads, "Man's life is laid in the loom of time/ To a pattern he does not see,/ While the weavers work and the shuttles fly/ Till the dawn of eternity."

intervene; listen constantly for the Holy Spirit's gentle voice.

An important part of this process is willingness to admit that you have made a wrong turn, and to ask God's help to get you back on the right road

> "It is pleasant to see plans develop. That is why fools refuse to give them up even when they are wrong."[261]

Also, if you do need supernatural guidance, don't be in a hurry; remember that even a Jeremiah had to wait on God-

> "After ten days, the word of the Lord came to Jeremiah."[262]

How different this prophet was from others, who angered God by their false predictions. Because they had no reply to his challenge, Jeremiah knew their oracles were untrue-

> "Who among you has ever approached the throne of God, to look upon him and to hear his word? Which one of you has ever listened for his voice, or heeded him when he spoke?"[263]

There is no discovery of the will of God apart from prayer.

UNITED WITH CHRIST

Successful guidance rests upon a relationship with Christ

---

[261] Proverbs 13:19, Living Bible.
[262] Jeremiah 42:7.
[263] 23:18. Note that the whole chapter deals with false prophets who claimed revelations from God that were actually their own invention.

strong enough to keep you secure, no matter what your present circumstances. The Shepherd Psalm begins with the joyful affirmation, "*I shall not want,*" yet contains the Valley of the Shadow of Death, and a Battle Field. The psalmist's trust was not in green pastures, nor still waters, but in the Lord himself. Likewise, *Christ* must be our goal, not health, nor prosperity, nor success, nor even heaven. Let him give us those things or take them away - whatever he pleases - only let nothing separate us from him! How can you be out of the will of God if you are in Christ? What can separate you from the Father's purpose if you are closely bonded to the Son?

Keep near to Jesus and you cannot go astray! You will live with an assurance that no matter how tortuous your path may be, the Father's hand is successfully carrying you on toward his appointed goal. Sir Thomas Browne, that urbane and gracious 17th century physician, whose words have several times adorned the above pages, spoke also on this matter. He describes two ways in which God relates to the world: the first *is according to steadfast and reliable law, such as the laws of nature, and of the spirit; the* second *is God's "unknown and secret way"* -

> *"There is another way, full of Meanders and Labyrinths, whereof the Devil and Spirits have no exact Ephemerides;*[264] *and that is a more particular and obscure method of his Providence, directing the operations of individuals and single Essences: this we call Fortune, that serpentine and crooked line, whereby he draws those actions his wisdom intends in a more unknown and secret way.*

---

[264] That is, no chart or map that would enable the Dark Powers to predict and interfere with the purpose of God.

This cryptic and involved method of his Providence have I ever admired; nor can I relate the History of my life, the occurrences of my days, the escapes of dangers, and hits of chance, with a Bezo las Manos[265] to Fortune, or a bare Gramercy[266] to my good Stars. Abraham might have thought the Ram in the thicket came thither by accident; humane reason would have said that mere chance conveyed Moses in the Ark to the sight of Pharaoh's Daughter: what a Labyrinth is there in the story of Joseph, able to convert a Stoick![267] Surely there are in every man's Life certain rubs, doublings, and wrenches, which pass a while under the effects of chance, but at the last, well examined, prove the mere hand of God."[268]

Theseus had less reason to trust his thread to lead him out of the Minoan maze than you and I have to trust the hand of God to guide us surely through the thickets of life. Whether he works before the event, or during or after it, the Lord remains indisputably in control of all that happens, and compels all things ultimately to contrive his pleasure.

THE ULTIMATE KEYS

All that I have said finally comes down to this: two noble

---

[265] A Spanish phrase meaning "a kiss of the hands" - that is, a casual acknowledgement, a careless salute to good luck.
[266] A surprised, but soon-forgotten, "Thank you!"
[267] That is, if he understood Divine Providence, the Stoic would turn from his philosophy of fatalism to trust in the goodness of God.
[268] Sir Thomas Browne: The Major Works; ed. by C. A. Patrides; Penguin Classics, London, 1977; "Religio Medici" pg. 81-82.

spiritual qualities provide the best keys to divine guidance -

(A) LOVE

If in every situation you do the most loving thing, that which best expresses love for God and for your neighbor, you will not go far wrong. The most reliable guidance springs out of a loving relationship with the Father through Christ, a relationship so intimate and constant that the mind of the Father is insensibly imparted to his child moment by moment.

I read somewhere that this is the difference between the gospel and magic. Heathen magic attempts to manipulate the gods, to make heaven subservient to human will; but humble Christians gladly submit to the will of God. Out of that surrender is born the relationship *the Father desires to establish with us through Christ; and out of that again springs a joyous* partnership *together in building the Kingdom, both now and for ever!*

(B) FAITH

To be in the will of God is primarily a matter of faith. If you agree with what you have read here, then with me you will be able to make these statements:

- since I am surrendered to God I trust that the decisions I make day by day are good, and that what I am doing is approved by him;
- there were probably other decisions I could have made that the Lord would have approved; but I am satisfied that he is pleased with the ones I have made;

- if I do not believe I am in the centre of God's will, then I will neither be there, nor can God bring me there; but if I do believe I am in the centre of his will, and affirm this confidently, then by the laws of faith I place upon God the burden of carrying me there! He cannot do other than honor real faith.

I believe I am in his will; therefore I am! I believe I serve him well; therefore I do! I believe I shall receive his crown; therefore I shall!

And if in any direction I have strayed from his path, I trust him to bring me where he wants me to be, and to make me what he wants me to be, and out of every bright noon or dark midnight to fulfill his wonderful purpose.

Epilogue

A NEW BEGINNING

I need to write one more chapter, both to complete this story and to set up a new beginning. I want to describe the greatest promise of answered prayer in the Bible.

In some ways the next few pages may seem to be a contradiction of things I have already written. That cannot be avoided - although "tension" might be a better word than "contradiction". If you read the Bible honestly, you will find that you cannot evade this tension, for it occurs everywhere in scripture. What is it? Simply the gap that exists between the extraordinary potential inherent in the promise of God and the often disappointing outworking of that promise in life. My earlier chapters have explored one side of this apparent contradiction. But I felt the book would not be complete without at least some statement of the other side!

The tension itself can be observed in many passages. Look again, for example, at the familiar 23rd Psalm. The poet begins with the peaceful line, *"The Lord is my Shepherd, I shall not want."* But he is not a fatalist. He does not believe that an affirmation of God as Shepherd means that the Lord controls, or even over-rules, every step he takes. So we notice a subtle change in the way he speaks. He says that *"the Lord gives me rest in green pastures, and leads me beside calm waters."* We expect him then to keep the same flow, and to say, *"he leads me also through the valley of the shadow of death."* Instead, he says, *"Even if I walk through the valley ..."*

Why this change of pronoun, from *"he"* to *"I"*?

Despite the psalmist's confidence in the shepherding care of God, he knows that life remains flexible and open. He can make choices of his own that sometimes bring him ruin and not prosperity; and life itself often takes unexpected twists and turns. Today's green and nourishing pastures may swiftly become tomorrow's grim chasm of death.

Nonetheless, he refuses to surrender this assurance: *so long as he can pray there remains hope of a miracle!* He knows that the Shepherd will never abandon him. He expects God to bring him *through* the valley, and into the bright sunshine of a new day, to more victories over his enemies, to an abundance of *"goodness and mercy"*.

So life with the Shepherd is not all verdant fields and laughing brooks; there are also enemies and perilous ravines, conflict with evil, battles to win, before our ultimate goal is reached.

The same tension between the promise of God and its outworking exists in other areas of faith. Think about the covenant of healing the Great Physician has made with his people. In a hundred places the Bible teaches us, in sickness, to trust God for healing.[269] Yet not all who call upon the Lord are healed. Despite fervent prayer, even fasting, many Christians die in the prime of life, ravaged by cancer, or by some other wretched illness.

---

[269] That is, if he understood Divine Providence, the Stoic would turn from his philosophy of fatalism to trust in the goodness of God.

Why is this so? Where is the promise of God? There are many explanations. We have to contend with numerous foes, which war against the fulfillment of the covenant: our own unbelief; Satanic opposition; worldliness and corruption in the church; a polluted natural environment; poor diet; deep unbelief in the community;[270] and the like.

Yet the potential remains, for those who can touch God in faith, to achieve vibrant good health, not just on the other side of the grave, but right now, in this life. The name of Jesus has power to destroy every disease![271]

Admittedly, after the resurrection of the dead, every believer is promised an utter fulfillment of every promise of God. But even now the latent power of the divine promise waits to be released by faith. Even now we can *"taste the powers of the coming kingdom of God"*.[272] So we are everywhere in scripture urged to stir up our faith, to reach for ever greater things from God, to expect signs, wonders, and miracles, to unlock ever mightier dimensions of answered prayer.

That is the theme of the rest of this chapter, and indeed, finally, of this entire book.

---

[270] Which baffled even Christ's healing ministry, Mark 6:5-6.
[271] See, for example, Mark 16:17-18; Acts 3:16.
[272] Hebrews 6:5.

EXCEEDING ABUNDANTLY

Nearly two hundred years ago the American inventor Robert Fulton constructed a submarine, which he offered to the French navy to use in their bitter war against the British. His invention was scorned by a French admiral, who declared: "I thank God, sir, France still fights her battles above the waves, not beneath them!"

Four years later, the British navy, under Lord Nelson, utterly crushed the French at the Battle of Trafalgar.

How different the world would be today if the French, using Fulton's invention, had won that battle!

Likewise, in the battles we wage on the seas of life, the best weapons are not those you hold visibly in your hand, but the hidden weapons of the heart.

Paul expresses that idea in a powerful benediction, which I will paraphrase a little -

> "God is able to do exceeding abundantly
> above all you can ask or think, according to
> the power that works within you!"[273]
>> Your God is able.
>> Your God is able to do what you ask.
>> Your God is able to do all *that you ask*.
>> Your God is able to do above *all that you ask*.
>> Your God is able to do abundantly *above all that you ask*.

---

[273] Ephesians 3:20.

> Your God is able to do exceeding
> abundantly above all that you ask.
> Your God is able to do exceeding
> abundantly above all that you ask or
> even think!

What shall we do with that extraordinary statement? Shall we call it wild hyperbole and ignore it? Is it a formal declaration of how much God wants to answer prayer, or is just a burst of pious enthusiasm? If Paul means us to take it literally, why do we see it so little fulfilled? After all, how many people do you know who get even a small part of their prayers answered in a minor way, let alone someone to whom God gives exceeding abundantly above all that he or she ever asked or even thought!

Is the fault with scripture? That seems hardly likely. So it must be with us. And indeed, Paul himself gives us the key to unlock this mystery. He uses the same Greek word to describe both our *working and* God's. *It is the word* dunamis, *which means* ability *or* power: "God is able to do ... according to the ability in you"; *or,* "God has power ... according to your power."

In other words, the exercise of divine ability depends upon the exercise of human ability; when you do what you are able to do, then God will do what he is able to do. You and I determine for ourselves how greatly the Lord works on our behalf. Or, to use Paul's words again, "According to the power/ability at work inside you, so God is able/has power to do exceeding abundantly above all you can ask or think."

We cannot escape that "according to"! It measures how much our prayers will be answered. According to the degree you stir up the ability, or power, that you possess within yourself, so God will stretch out his hand to do as you ask.

What is this "power/ability" that lies within us?

I suppose many answers could be given to that question, but here I want to confine myself to three of them

THE POWER OF DECISION

This much we can all do: make a decision! What decision? The decision to pray boldly and to expect great answers to our prayers. You must face this spiritual demand: you will have mighty answers to prayer only when you decide to have them. The choice is not God's, but yours. The Father has already made his decision. He has already told us in scripture how willing he is to do incredible things for his children. Unanswered prayer is not God's fault. He is more than willing to do more than we ask! But because we expect so little, we get so little. The ball, as they say in the classics, is now in your court. Will you just poke at it, or give it a mighty swipe?

Perhaps someone says, "What does it matter? Why should I put myself to the trouble of stirring up faith, of breaking through the barriers, of treading Satan under foot, just to pray better than I have been doing?" For several very important reasons -

You have needs that only great answers to great prayers can meet. How will you ever see the fulfillment of the promises of God in your daily life - promises that embrace your material, moral, and spiritual needs - unless you stop sitting, and waiting, and decide that NOW is the time for God to start giving you "exceedingly abundant" answers to your prayers?

You have a call that only great answers to great prayers can empower." Every believer is called to experience the glory of God, to walk in holiness, to achieve excellence in Christ.[274] Never be content with mediocrity! Never think you have gone far enough in faith! Emulate Paul, and say to yourself, "I have not yet obtained God's best, I have not yet reached perfection; so I will press on toward the heavenly goal, straining for the prize of God's highest call in Christ!"[275]

You have a duty that only great answers to great prayers can fulfill." Can anyone suppose that God can be served, Christ can be revealed, the church be increased, by natural skill alone? How foolish! There are walls too high to leap, and enemies too numerous to overcome, without God's supernatural help.[276] The natural man unaided can never serve God effectively. Whatever we do for the Lord must be done in the strength of the Lord. In the end, nothing is worth doing that is not done as an answer to prayer. Only by prayer that infuses our labor with God's own miraculous touch can our works of straw be turned into "gold, silver, and priceless gems"![277]

How willing is God to give great answers to great prayers? Our text answers that question in a special way. When Paul said "God is able", *he used a phrase in Greek which is active, not passive nor abstract. It describes not merely a potential, or possibility, of power, but something*

---

[274] 2 Peter 1:3-4.
[275] Philippians 3:12-14.
[276] Psalm 18:29, and see also 34-39; etc.
[277] 1 Corinthians 3:12-15.

that is actually happening. He is telling us, not just who God is (the All-Powerful-One), but what God does (he works All-Powerfully)! That is, somewhere in the world today God is now doing exceeding abundantly above all you could ask or think. If he is doing it there, why not here? If he is doing it for them, why not for us? The choice is yours!

THE POWER OF PERSISTENCE

The Queen Mother, Queen Elizabeth, who is 90 years of age as I write, is perhaps the best-loved person in the United Kingdom. She has earned that love by her dauntless courage and nobility of character. During the London Blitz she was asked whether the little princesses (Elizabeth and Margaret Rose) would be taken out of the country to safety -perhaps to Australia or Canada. She replied: "The children will not leave unless I do. I shall not leave until their father does; and the king will not leave the country under any circumstances whatever."

Courageous persistence is a virtue often admired in scripture.[278] But this is just what is lacking in many Christians. They perhaps make a good decision to dare more greatly in the Lord, but they falter in their follow-up. It is not enough just to begin well, we must also finish well.

Yet how often the servants of the Lord are impatient, not strong, not bold, not determined. Learn this lesson: if you want to possess *then you must* persist! *As long as you have life and breath, never give up, never yield to doubt, nor surrender to fear. Keep praying. Keep believing. Keep*

---

[278] For just two examples, see 1 Corinthians 15:58; 16:16:13.

hoping. Keep reaching for God's exceeding abundance!

Someone says: it's too late for me; despite earnest prayer, my child has already died. Then seize a different answer: show an extraordinary joy in the presence of death; display the magnificent triumph of Christ over the grave; refuse to allow the devil any place of victory in your bereavement; declare yourself more than a conqueror over the enemy's darkest power.

Someone says: what use is prayer to me; my business is already ruined; I have lost my house, my money, my prosperity; I stand bankrupt. Then get a new promise, build a new hope, start a new venture; learn from your mistakes, clamber up to a new pinnacle of faith, regain all that you have lost, and more. You have a good example in Job, who got back double what Satan stole from him![279]

Someone says: I cried out to the Lord to help me, but heaven was deaf; now my life is ruined by sin, my character destroyed, my name disgraced, my friends ashamed to own me. Or another: what chance is there for me, decayed by drugs and alcohol, defeated again and again; why add more futile prayers to those of the past?

But you should *never* give up! Persist in prayer! Keep hoping, keep asking. Remember Paul, who prayed earnestly *"night and day"*[280] against apparently insurmountable barriers. He refused to accept defeat. He knew the answer lay in God. He knew that dauntless prayer would bring him whatever miracle it took to meet his need. The greatest part of faith is persistence. Hold fast your confidence. Never throw it away. If you press

---

[279] Job 42:10.
[280] 1 Thessalonians 3:10.

on bravely, an answer, a great answer, will surely come![281]

THE POWER OF THE HOLY SPIRIT

Translators remain unsure just how to word our text in Ephesians 3:20. Paul used a Greek construction that can be expressed in two ways: one is called "middle"; the other "passive".

If the middle construction is used, the text will read, "according to the power at work within us" -that is, this "power" is something that we ourselves possess and must put to use; it arises from within our own being. This is the way I have been using the text so far: stir up your own ability to choose, to pray, to believe, to persist.

But if the passive construction is used, the text will read, "according to the power that enables us" - that is, this power is now something that comes upon us from the outside, and carries us beyond ourselves, way past our own limited abilities. This reading points to the Holy Spirit, pouring into us the very might of heaven, equipping us to do the will of God exceeding abundantly!

How much we need that enabling! Are we not all confined by fences that are not of our desire or making? Everywhere you turn, you find someone trying to lock you into their expectations, their will, their opinion of who you are and what you can do. No one ever thinks as well of you as God does! The Father always reckons you can do more, much more, than the world reckons you can.

Just let someone try to break away from mediocrity and to reach a higher plane than their neighbors have dared

---
[281] Hebrews 10:36-39.

to dream possible. At once the clamorous, condemning, timorous voices sound: "Who do you think you are? How proud can you get! Climb back into the box with us! Get back into your hole! We can't endure you becoming better than we are, going further, getting more!" You will hear those voices in the world, and perhaps even more in the church. Imprisoning, suffocating, blockading voices; eager to tell you what can't be done, rather than to provoke you to faith and to splendid accomplishments in Christ.

Then also, the devil will knock you down whenever he can, mocking your faith, scorning your efforts, whispering words of ruin into your soul. And if that were not enough, there is also the voice of your own fallen flesh, resisting the gospel call to righteousness, telling you that you will never be any better, or wiser, or stronger than you are.

A *physician* diagnoses your disease as incurable, and locks you into a prison of death: but *your God is able to do exceeding abundantly above all you can ask or think*! So call for the elders of the church, pray the prayer of faith, and expect a miracle![282]

A *financier* pronounces you bankrupt, and condemns you to poverty: but *your God is able to do exceeding abundantly above all you can ask or think*! So ask him, and keep on asking him, to meet your need abundantly, according to his great riches in Christ in the heavenlies![283]

An *employer* declares you inept, and crushes your dream of higher attainment: but *your God is able to do exceeding abundantly above all you can ask or think*! So meditate in

---

[282] James 5:14-15.
[283] Philippians 4:19.

his word day and night until you are bold to grasp the promise of fruitfulness and prosperity![284]

A *counselor* says your habit is too ingrained, you will never overcome it: *but your God is able to do exceeding abundantly above all you can ask or think*! So rise up in Jesus' name, tread down those serpents and scorpions, and proclaim yourself more than a conqueror in Christ![285]

A *neighbor* scoffs at your aspiration to achieve great things for God, and insists you will never be any different from what you have always been: but *your God is able to do exceeding abundantly above all you can ask or think*! So break loose from mediocrity. You can change! You can find a new strength, a new vision, a new direction, a new vitality in Christ![286]

The *devil* whispers in your ear that God is against you, that you will never amount to anything in his sight, that you might as well accept your inferiority, your weakness, your failure: but *your God is able to do exceeding abundantly above all you can ask or think*! So push the Accuser away; declare that God is for you and has never been against you, and that you will go on to fulfill everything the Father has given you to do![287]

Walls! How many walls people try to build around us!

But thank God, he has acted in Christ to smash down every one of those walls, and to open before every Spirit-filled saint a vista of boundless opportunity! See how Paul

---

[284] Psalm 1:1-3.
[285] Luke 10:19; Romans 8:37; Philippians 4:13.
[286] 2 Corinthians 5:17; Ephesians 1:16-19.
[287] Romans 8:31-34; John 15:16.

describes this joyous freedom -

> *"Wherever the Spirit of the Lord dwells, there is liberty, so that we ... are being constantly changed from glory to glory!"*[288]

What is the call of God? Ever to advance from glory, to glory, to glory! Where the Spirit of the Lord reigns, boundaries are destroyed, horizons are expanded, doors are opened, valleys become pathways to the mountain top. Here is the Bible description of a proper Christian life: *from glory to glory*! Today better than yesterday; tomorrow richer than today. Ever onward, ever upward, toward the blazing splendor of the Lord himself. No plains, no plateaus; just a steady, glad ascent toward heaven's ultimate bliss.

Why then all these gloomy saints, whose yesterdays sparkled more brightly than the present hour? They wince at the enthusiasm of young Christians, drearily predicting that this fresh zeal will not last. They throw spiteful buckets of water over eager young joy, determined to freeze every new convert into their own chilly unbelief. They simply condemn themselves as people who have lost their first love.[289]

That great orator and saint of the early 5th century, John Chrysostom, described well such frigid Christians -

> *"But what (does it mean), `we reflecting as a mirror the glory of the Lord, are transformed into the same image'? ... (As) soon as we are baptized, the soul beameth even more than*

---

[288] 2 Corinthians 3:17-18.
[289] Revelation 2:1-7.

the sun, being cleansed by the Spirit; and not only do we behold the glory of God, but from it also receive a sort of splendor ... Wherefore also he saith, `Reflecting as a mirror we are transformed into the same image from glory' - that of the Spirit - `to glory' -our own, that which is generated in us; and that of such sort as one might expect from the Lord the Spirit ...

"Woe is me! For well is it that we should here even groan bitterly, for that we who enjoy a birth so noble do not so much as know what is said, because we quickly lose the reality, and are dazzled about the objects of sense. For this glory, the unspeakable and awful, remaineth in us for a day or two, and then we quench it, bringing over it the winter of worldly concerns, and with the thickness of those clouds repelling its rays.

"For worldly things are a winter, and than winter more lowering. For not frost is engendered thence, nor rain, neither doth it produce mire and deep swamps; but, things than all these more grievous, it formeth hell and the miseries of hell. And as in severe frost the limbs are stiffened and are dead, so truly the soul shuddering in the winter of sins also, performeth none of its proper functions, stiffened as it were, by a frost, as to conscience."[290]

Let the Holy Spirit thaw those frosts! Let him carry you

---

[290] The passage comes from a sermon John preached on the text we are considering, 2 Corinthians 3:17-18. The Nicene and Post-Nicene Fathers, Vol 12; pg. 314.

from glory to glory. No matter how many skirmishes you may have lost, the war is still on, and absolute victory still beckons.

Have you prayed and failed?

Then pray again and succeed. Never give up!

So long as you refuse to let go of Christ and of your hope in him, you cannot finally be defeated. Your eventual triumph is absolutely assured, if not this side of the grave, then certainly on the other side.

That of, course, is the ultimate focus of our hope. The consummation of our faith will be in heaven, before the Father's throne, surrounded by the acclamations of the angels. There our text also will find its most magnificent fulfillment.

Wonderful as the things may be that the Lord does for his people on earth, they are dust compared with the brilliance of what he has prepared in heaven.[291] There truly we will see how our God has done for us exceeding abundantly above all we asked or ever dared to think.

How measureless is his grace and power! It surpasses all our thought:

- we never thought we could *survive death*: but already we feel the throb of resurrection power in Christ, and we know that death has lost all its sting.[292]
- we never thought we could *escape the grave*: but our

---

[291] 1 Corinthians 2:9.
[292] 1 Corinthians 15:51-57.

rising feet will shake off its very dust when Jesus comes and calls us to meet him the air.[293]
- we never thought we could be *clothed with beauty*: but now we are destined to be transformed into the likeness of Jesus himself when we see him in his glory.[294]
- we never thought we could be *equal with the angels*: but now we bear the honor of those who are appointed by God to judge the heavenly host.[295]
- we never thought we could *reign with Christ*: but now we hear the promise of sitting with him on his throne to rule the nations with a rod of iron.[296]
- we never thought we could *possess the kingdom*: but now we are made co-heirs with Christ of all that exists, in heaven and on earth.[297]
- we never thought we could be happy for ever: but now we are comforted by the promise that all sorrow will be forgotten, all tears wiped away, and that we shall share the joy of Christ for ever.[298]

Can you any longer deny it? Both in time and eternity **our God is able to do exceeding <u>abundantly above all we can ask or think!</u>**

---

[293] 1 Thessalonians 4:13-18.
[294] 1 John 3:1-3; and compare Revelation 1:12-16 for a suggestion of how Christ may look when he comes.
[295] 1 Corinthians 6:2-3.
[296] Revelation 2:26-29.
[297] Romans 8:15-17.
[298] Revelation 21:1-7.

Addendum

PRAYER AND GOD'S FOREKNOWLEDGE

INTRODUCTION

Like Amos, I might say that I am neither a prophet nor the son of a prophet. Unlike him, I cannot claim any kind of divine infallibility for the ideas I present. Nonetheless I am going to attempt a difficult task. I am going to pretend that I am a philosopher, and under this guise discuss the problem of how answered prayer relates to God's foreknowledge of all events. After all, if God knows everything that is going to happen, and if the future is fixed by him, why bother to pray? Prayer would seem a futile exercise.

This dilemma has perplexed many people. Some have even stopped praying, or pray only as a matter of formal routine. The question is: *does God's foreknowledge and immutability make answered prayer impossible?* Does prayer change God, or does it change us? Does it change anything?

I cannot attempt a full discussion of these issues; in fact I will do no more than make a series of statements touching on some aspects of the problem. My purpose is to offer guidelines for you to develop further (if you wish to do so) by your own thinking and study, or perhaps by discussion with others.

The question again is: *"Does God's foreknowledge and immutability make answered prayer impossible?"*

(1) The question is based on the idea that answered prayer must involve a change in the future that might have been, or in the future God has decreed, or in the future as God presently knows it. But scripture says that God is immutable: *"I am the Lord, I change not!"* If God cannot be changed, if God foreknows the future (which, it is said, must fix the future in the form in which God presently knows it) how can prayer be answered in any real sense of the word? Surely God's foreknowledge and immutability must mean either:

-   that prayer is merely a devotional exercise, without any real power to change anything; or, if prayer does have power to change things, then

-   that God has predetermined the time and content of our prayers so that the answering of them does not cause any disruption of his program.

This means prayer loses either its *voluntary character*, or its *effective power*. It seems impossible that prayer should remain both voluntary and powerful; for if it is both, then the future is continually being changed, depending on whether or not we choose to pray.

However, this argument is true only if God has decreed himself unwilling to change future events, or to change his purpose, in answer to prayer. But in fact scripture shows he is willing to do both, and this is part of his immutable character. Here are some examples:

-the repentance of Nineveh changed God's announced intention of destroying the city within forty days (Jonah 3:3-10)

-God was prepared to annihilate Israel, and to begin a new national program through Moses, but Moses stayed the Lord's hand (Exodus 32:9-14; Numbers 14:11-20; cp also Psalm 106:40-46; Jeremiah 18:7-10; Joel 2:12-14; Matthew 23:37-39.)

-Micah announced the ruin of Jerusalem, but because the people repented, the disaster was averted for a full one hundred years (Jeremiah 26:16-19; cp also vs. 1-6).

(2) Concerning God's knowledge of the future: the future God knows is one that includes the answer to our prayers. If we don't pray, the future God knows is a future void for us of an answer to prayer.

Science fiction writers have grappled with a similar problem in their attempt to describe what might happen if a traveler were able to go back in time and change some significant event in the past (for example, prevent the birth of Napoleon, or cause Nazi Germany to win the battle of Stalingrad).

It is generally assumed that for a future observer the past that had been would be at once changed, and all memory of it would vanish, to be replaced by the memory of a newly created past.

(3) The future belongs to man, not God. God has no future. He dwells in an eternal present. Only man is advancing into the future. The future is part of the human condition, not the divine. We dwell in a time/space

continuum, but God dwells in eternity (Isaiah 57:15).

The future as such is not decreed by God (at least not in detail); it is the sum total of human activity. I will comment more on this in statement (5), but in general it may be said that the future God knows is a future determined by our actions, plus the degree of divine involvement invited or demanded by human righteousness or iniquity. We cannot adopt a fatalistic stance and avoid the responsibility of action.

(4) We are largely the masters of our own destiny. It lies within the prerogative of the human race to change its own future because the future is open-ended. It is a mistake to view the future in the same way we view the past.

The science fiction writers are wrong: the past is immutable, even to God. But the future *is* mutable. If man does one day learn to travel through time he will only ever be able to go forward, to hasten the clock, but never to turn it back (even when Hezekiah's sun-dial retreated ten degrees, time itself still continued its relentless advance). The past is fixed and forever unchangeable. Indeed, there is no such *thing* as the past. What we call "the past" is nothing more than a memory or record of events that once happened.

Neither is the future a self-existent entity. It is not created by a decree of God. The future has no existence apart from man. It is the product of human activity, intermingled with occasional acts of divine intervention.

(5) God has decreed, or fixed the future only in the following sense -

(a) His kingdom will come and his will be done; but the fact that we are commanded to *pray* for this shows that the time and the manner are flexible in the purpose of God.

The coming of *"the last day"* and of the hour of judgment are conditioned also by the Lord's desire to bring many sons to glory. His principle is not to *hasten* the last day, but rather to delay it as long as possible.

(b) He has said that a certain set of conditions on earth will evoke an inevitable response from heaven. So, *"when the iniquity of the Amorites was full"*, the wrath of God devoured them; or, when the Lord observes faith, he hastens to fulfill his promise to the one believing.

(c) Biblical prophecy is sufficiently flexible, or sufficiently open in its form, to allow God room to maneuver.

(d) God has so structured the universe that he is able to achieve his full purpose (and will achieve it) without restricting human freedom of choice.

(e) God is always free to intervene in present human affairs and to order events in conformity with his will (Isaiah 55:11; Psalm 135:6).

Other Books By The Author

Authenticity & Authority of the Bible

Building the Church God Wants

Clothed with Power

The Cross and the Crown

Dynamic Christian Foundations

Mountain Movers

Strong Reasons

Throne Rights

Understanding Your Bible

For a full list of the authors books visit:

www.visionpublishingservices.com

Dr. Ken Chant

www.ingramcontent.com/pod-product-compliance
Lightning Source LLC
Chambersburg PA
CBHW070726160426
43192CB00009B/1338